WRITERS AND THEIR WORK

ISOBEL ARMSTRONG
General Editor

FLANN O'BRIEN

© The Irish Times

FLANN O'BRIEN

FLANN
O'BRIEN

Joseph Brooker

for the Brother

© Copyright 2005 by Joseph Brooker

First published in 2005 by Northcote House Publishers Ltd, Horndon, Tavistock, Devon, PL19 9NQ, United Kingdom.
Tel: +44 (01822) 810066. Fax: +44 (01822) 810034.

All rights reserved. No part of this work may be reproduced or stored in an information retrieval system (other than short extracts for the purposes of review) without the express permission of the Publishers given in writing.

British Library Cataloguing-in-Publication Data
A catalogue record for this book is available from the British Library

ISBN 0-7463-1081-1 hardback
ISBN 0-7463-1013-7 paperback

Typeset by TW Typesetting, Plymouth, Devon
Printed and bound in the United Kingdom by
Athenaeum Press Ltd., Gateshead, Tyne & Wear

Contents

Biographical Outline

1911   5 October: born Brian O'Nolan, Strabane, (Northern) Ireland. Family spend a brief period in Glasgow.

1916   Easter Rising, Dublin: O'Nolan family are living in the Dublin suburb Inchicore.

1917   O'Nolan family return to Strabane.

1922   James Joyce's *Ulysses* published in Paris.

1923   The family move permanently to Dublin. O'Nolan is educated by Christian Brothers at Synge Street School.

1929   October: Brian O'Nolan begins studies at University College Dublin.

1932   Gains BA degree with honours in German, English and Irish.

1935   Gains MA from UCD for his thesis on 'Nature in Irish Poetry'. Enters Civil Service (Department of Local Government) – known variously as Nolan, O'Nolan, and Ó Nualláin.

1939   'Flann O'Brien' publishes first novel, *At Swim-Two-Birds*. Joyce publishes *Finnegans Wake*. World War II breaks out.

1940   Second novel, *The Third Policeman*, rejected by Longman and left unpublished in O'Nolan's lifetime.
        4 October: first 'Cruiskeen Lawn' column by 'Myles na gCopaleen' appears in the *Irish Times*.

1941   'Myles na gCopaleen' publishes *An Béal Bocht* (posthumous English translation: *The Poor Mouth*). Death of James Joyce.

1942–3 Writes the plays *Thirst*, *Faustus Kelly* and *The Insect Play*, which are staged at Dublin's Gate, Abbey and Gaiety Theatres respectively.

1948   2 December: marries Evelyn McDonnell.
1951   US edition of *At Swim-Two-Birds*.
1953   Retirement from Civil Service, officially for health reasons. Commences additional newspaper columns for newspapers outside Dublin.
1954   Organizes unofficial 50th anniversary celebration of Bloomsday.
1960   *At Swim-Two-Birds* republished in London.
1961   Publishes *The Hard Life*. Writes television scripts.
1964   Publishes *The Dalkey Archive*; it is performed as *The Saints Go Cycling In* at the Gate Theatre. Begins work on *Slattery's Sago Saga*.
1966   1 April: Brian O'Nolan dies.
1967   *The Third Policeman* published.
1968   *The Best of Myles* published: first in a series of *Cruiskeen Lawn* reprints.
1975   First academic study of all his work appears.
1986   Flann O'Brien Symposium in Dublin.

Abbreviations

Works by Flann O'Brien

AS   *At Swim-Two-Birds* (Harmondsworth: Penguin, 1967)
AW   *Flann O'Brien At War: Myles na gCopaleen 1940–1945*, ed. John Wyse Jackson (London: Duckworth, 1999)
BM   *The Best of Myles* ed. Kevin O'Nolan (London: Picador, 1977)
DA   *The Dalkey Archive* (London: Flamingo, 1993)
FC   *Further Cuttings From Cruiskeen Lawn* (London: Grafton, 1988)
HL   *The Hard Life* (London: Picador, 1976)
MBM   *Myles Before Myles*, ed. John Wyse Jackson (London: Grafton, 1988)
PM   *The Poor Mouth*, trans. Patrick C. Power (London: Flamingo, 1993)
SP   *Stories and Plays* (London: Paladin, 1991)
TP   *The Third Policeman* (London: Flamingo, 1993)

Works about Flann O'Brien

FOB   Anne Clissmann, *Flann O'Brien: A Critical Introduction to his Writings* (Dublin: Gill & Macmillan, 1975)
IB   Peter Costello and Peter van de Kamp, *Flann O'Brien: An Illustrated Biography* (London: Bloomsbury, 1987)
NLM   Anthony Cronin, *No Laughing Matter: The Life and Times of Flann O'Brien* (London: Grafton, 1989)

Introduction: The Morning After

Flann O'Brien didn't exist, but fortunately someone invented him. That was Brian O'Nolan (1911–1966), a man from the North of Ireland who made himself a Dubliner – made himself, even, *the* Dubliner of his generation. O'Nolan – Ó Nualláin, to give him the Irish name which he never quite allowed to dwindle into disuse – first demonstrated his prodigious comic talent in his days as a student at University College, Dublin. As a graduate, he developed more than one career simultaneously. He put food on the table – for his family as well as himself, following his father's death – by working in Ireland's Civil Service. Meanwhile, he attempted to become an author of experimental fiction: a bid which succeeded brilliantly but all too briefly. The first book by 'Flann O'Brien', *At Swim-Two-Birds* (1939), was hailed by other modern writers as a remarkable debut: yet when his second novel, *The Third Policeman*, was rejected by a London publisher in 1941, O'Nolan feared that his career as a novelist was at an end. Fortunately – perhaps fortunately – he had another creative outlet to hand. From 1940 he had been writing a regular newspaper column in the *Irish Times*: and for more than two decades he devoted himself to this job as well as to the Civil Service, from which he was retired in 1953. By the 1960s O'Nolan was an alcoholic, increasingly prone to illness and hospitalization. Yet it was at this point that his career took a final surprising turn. In 1960 *At Swim-Two-Birds* was reissued in London: and O'Nolan, seemingly inspired by this vote of confidence, mustered the energy to begin writing fiction again. Two novels, *The Hard Life*

1

(1961) and *The Dalkey Archive* (1964), appeared before his early death in 1966.

At the time of his death O'Nolan was a cult figure at best. His newspaper column, *Cruiskeen Lawn*, was his greatest source of fame in Ireland, and his reputation abroad was patchy. But in the three decades and more which have passed since then, his work has edged into prominence, even into the literary canon. In 1967 the surviving manuscript of *The Third Policeman* was found among his papers, and the novel was published at last. The book has joined *At Swim-Two-Birds* as a demonstration of the remarkable gifts of the young O'Nolan. Both novels have also taken on a new life as exemplary literary experiments: anti-novels and verbal games to rank alongside the work of such international figures as Vladimir Nabokov, Italo Calvino, or Jorge Luis Borges (who actually reviewed *At Swim* in 1939). Theorists of postmodernism in the novel point to Flann O'Brien as a key figure: and other writers continue to draw inspiration from him.[1] At the same time, like many of his compatriots, O'Nolan is beginning to be assessed within the particular historical and geographical context in which he worked. In the 1980s and 1990s, discussion of such modern Irish writers as W. B. Yeats, James Joyce and Samuel Beckett has sought to restore the question of Ireland to their work. Critics have been asking what imprint its particular history made on their writing, and – conversely – what their writing made of Ireland.[2] The same questions might be asked of Brian O'Nolan, in his various guises.

One reason that O'Nolan's work has taken a while to receive its due is that so much of it was done outside the literary forms which dominate the modern canon: the novel, poetry and drama. Indeed, a writer who evades all three of these genres would be lucky to get labelled as 'literature' at all. O'Nolan wrote in all three. He produced five novels, which might all fit inside one of the fatter editions of *Ulysses*. He translated poetry from the Irish, with a lightness of touch which has been praised by bilingual readers. And he attempted to become a successful playwright: in 1943 three of his plays were performed in Dublin. Yet O'Nolan's assembled output in these genres is dwarfed by the amount he wrote outside them:

chiefly in comic and satirical newspaper columns, and above all in the *Cruiskeen Lawn* under the name Myles na gCopaleen. This work is still in the process of collection and publication. A generous selection of the early columns, *The Best of Myles*, was produced in 1968, and has been supplemented by further volumes. One of these, *Myles Away From Dublin*, contains a selection from a quite different column written for the *Nationalist and Leinster Times*, under the new alias of George Knowall. And to cap this, there is the diverse work produced before the personae of Flann O'Brien or Myles na gCopaleen had been conceived. Much of O'Nolan's writing for the student journal *Comhthrom Féinne*, in the first half of the 1930s, and the brief but brilliant magazine *Blather* in 1934–5, is the equal of his later work, and has been made available in John Wyse Jackson's collection *Myles Before Myles* (1988). We are dealing with a writer who was more or less a novelist, but also – depending on your point of view – more than, or less than, a novelist.

So the existing canons of literary criticism have not really known what to do with a lot of O'Nolan's best work, unless it be to relegate it to a lightweight world of 'humour' somewhere below the proper gaze of literary judgement. The last twenty years have seen significant challenges to the canon. These challenges have affected its content, with new attention being given to previously unconsidered writers, many of them from historically marginalized groups. They have also dented the very concept of the canon, which is often held to be a hierarchical and reductive category no matter who gets into it. The gradually increasing repute of Brian O'Nolan may have had something to do with these challenges – may reflect a new readiness to consider the merits of those modes of writing whose claims to full literary status are tenuous. But in O'Nolan's case, the full implications of this have not yet been articulated. He remains, unlike some of the twentieth century's greatest writers, harder to classify than to read, a figure whose less conventionally literary work has yet to find a secure home in literature. This need not be a bad thing. I suggest – and I shall seek to show in this book – that one reason why O'Nolan remains such a compelling figure is the difficulty of pinning him down. His ambiguous literary status – and the uncertainty which he himself appears to have experienced over

3

what kind of writer he was, or wanted to be – are among the reasons he fascinates today.

Another reason is his elusiveness. Hugh Kenner once opened an essay with the mock-tentative suggestion 'Let us begin by assuming Samuel Beckett's existence';[3] but we cannot quite begin by assuming Flann O'Brien's existence. The author of *At Swim-Two-Birds* is best known by that name, but he did little to clarify the matter of authorship with the letter that he wrote to the *Irish Press* in 1939, in which he disclaimed authorship of a book rumoured to be 'objectionable, even if non-existent' (*MBM* 178). In the novel itself, the novelist William Tracy invents the practice of 'aestho-autogamy', in which literary characters are born fully grown and in their twenties, on the basis that 'Many social problems of contemporary interest . . . could be readily resolved if issue could be born already matured, teethed, reared, educated, and ready to essay those competitive plums which make the Civil Service and the Banks so attractive to the younger breadwinners of today' (*AS* 41). It is therefore appropriate that Flann O'Brien should have been, as his commentator Robert Tracy says, 'born on 13 March 1939, on the title page of *At Swim-Two-Birds*'.[4] The author is artefact as well as source.

'Flann O'Brien', O'Nolan explained to his publisher prior to *At Swim*'s publication, 'has the advantage that it contains an unusual name and one that is quite ordinary' (*NLM* 88). In that sense it resembles much of his work, which – all the way to the late novels of the 1960s – frequently plays on the collision of the mundane and the fantastic. It is the name that the world most frequently attaches to O'Nolan: it is taken by most books on the writer, including this one. I shall not, however, refer to him as 'O'Brien' throughout, because I want to register the multiplicity of his names, and the elusiveness of the personality that this implies. In a late article bearing the name Myles na Gopaleen, O'Nolan at last discussed this directly:

> the compartmentation of . . . personality for the purpose of literary utterance ensures that the fundamental individual will not be credited with a certain way of thinking, fixed attitudes, irreversible techniques of expression. No author should write under his own

name nor under one permanent pen-name; a male writer should
include in his impostures a female pen-name, and possibly vice
versa. (*NLM* 225)

The purpose of pen-names, it seems, is to protect the real self
beneath them – to protect it, specifically, from falling into fixed
modes of expression, from being typecast. Whether Brian
O'Nolan himself managed to avoid a certain ossification of the
personality is doubtful. He would sometimes refer to his
personae as discrete individuals: when Anthony Cronin suggested, in the 1950s, that he publish a novel under the old
name 'Flann O'Brien', O'Nolan replied 'I don't know that
fellow any longer' (*NLM* 197). But writer and persona might
not be so swiftly dissociated, especially in the case of the
persona in which he lived longest: Myles na gCopaleen. John
Wyse Jackson's formulation is elegant: 'For the first ten years,
say, between 1930 and 1940, he was seeking a voice. During the
next ten years or so, he had found it. After about 1950, he had
become that voice' (*MBM* 8). The mask of Myles became
harder and harder to remove, to distinguish from any under-
lying face.
   To put this more positively: the identity of this writer does
not reside simply in his brute reality, the curmudgeon whose
appearance demystifies all his aliases out of existence. The
aliases are part of the identity: in a sense O'Nolan became
more himself, and more than himself, in writing. He found his
voice by putting on voices: he enjoyed himself by making up
selves. Just how many names there were is uncertain –
and the uncertainty is of course a direct result of the mystifying
multiplicity. For instance, O'Nolan's possible authorship of
detective novels under the name Stephen Blakesley – an author
whose publishers knew him as Francis Bond – remains deeply
uncertain.[5] O'Nolan certainly performed in the letter columns
of the *Irish Times* (a phenomenon we shall examine in the next
chapter), but uncertainty remains over which letters were
penned by him, rather than his friends. Even the spelling of
names seems to multiply them. Flann O'Brien appeared in the
press as 'F O'Brien'; Myles na gCopaleen became Myles na
Gopaleen; Brian O'Nolan was sometimes Brian Nolan. In 1935
he sat the entrance examination for the Civil Service as 'Brian

'Ó Nualláin'; but the report for his first day at work stated that 'Mr Nolan reported for duty today' (*NLM* 79). When he made an official complaint about being addressed as 'Nolan', he remarked that 'My own name is one of the few subjects upon which I claim to be an authority' (*NLM* 78). It became the kind of subject upon which one *could* be an authority.

It is thus peculiarly tricky to read back from the work to the man. The facts of his life itself are disputed to a remarkable degree, frequently thanks to his own efforts in laying false trails. In 1943 he told a journalist from *Time* magazine that during a trip to Germany ten years earlier, he had married a violin-playing German girl, Clara Ungerland. 'She died a month later', the article recorded: 'O'Nolan returned to Eire and never mentions her'. He subsequently denied that she had ever existed, characteristically delighting in having fooled an American. His biographers, though, are unable to agree on the matter, or on when he went to Germany, if indeed he went at all.[6] Sue Asbee records visits to New York in 1944; Anthony Cronin, a friend of O'Nolan's, writes that the German visit was 'probably the only journey outside Ireland he ever made' (*NLM* 70). Even his death, falling as it did on April Fool's Day, was initially received as a jest by some acquaintances (*IB* 140): such was the unreliable status of fact in this writer's life.

Myles na gCopaleen, as Cronin observes, 'will usually be found . . . on several sides of a question at once' (*NLM* 124). In public quarrels, his antagonists can often be observed attacking the disguise. Sean O'Faolain, targeted by O'Nolan's satire in the late 1930s, disparaged 'Flann O'Brien' as 'the man in the Gaelic mask' (*NLM* 107). O'Nolan was not the first Irish writer to call to mind such an image. 'Man is least himself', wrote Oscar Wilde five decades earlier, 'when he talks in his own person. Give him a mask and he will tell you the truth'.[7] More thoroughly and vividly than any of his late nineteenth-century contemporaries, Wilde developed and aired the idea that the self was a kind of fiction, a series of poses: a matter of art rather than nature. His compatriot W. B. Yeats formed his own doctrine of the mask to describe his sense of identity. As Richard Ellmann notes, it 'includes all the differences between one's own and other people's conception of one's personality. To be conscious of the discrepancy which makes a mask of this sort is to look at oneself as if one were somebody else'. The mask, Ellmann adds, has martial qualities: it is a defensive armour for the self, and a 'weapon of attack' which exalts the self's capacities.[8] It is hard to think of a more different artist from Yeats than Brian O'Nolan: but the image of the mask is recast in O'Nolan's career. The self-dramatizing subjectivity of Yeats, with its collection of enigmatic and heroic poses, finds a comical echo in O'Nolan, with his bank of ridiculous personae.

If anything, O'Nolan's writing outstrips the sense of artifice already present in these precursors. Like them, he uses the mask – the persona – to assert the self and to disguise it simultaneously. It hides the self, works as armour: but it also facilitates extravagant attacks and polemical grandstanding. But the residual romanticism of his Protestant precursors is stripped from O'Nolan's practice. Give a man a mask and he'll tell the truth, said Wilde; give a man a mask, imply the pages of the *Irish Times*, and he'll lie more entertainingly than usual. O'Nolan lacks the aestheticist doctrine of Wilde: his only guide is pragmatic, the number of pen-names an author should have at his disposal, like fake passports in the event of a quick getaway. Yet O'Nolan practises the dissolution of the self in his writing in a purer fashion than Wilde. Rather than the honing of a persona of perfect wit and sensitivity, his writing offers a series of voices, caricatures, accents, discourses. We have moved, historically, from the religion of art to its parodic denigration: yet the forging of writerly identity has become more, not less, central.

Brian O'Nolan thus prefigures the scepticism about the self which would become more prevalent later in the century. By the 1980s, the American theorist Fredric Jameson could suggest that the 'depth model' of thought was on the wane, replaced by a 'multiplicity of surfaces'.[9] The human subject, in this climate, is conceived less as a source of thought and action, more as a blank canvas on which the surrounding culture paints. Or perhaps as a series of performances: masks behind which lies no authentic face. In this sense, O'Nolan's writing now looks ahead of its time. The self-consciousness of his early novels, and his cavalier attitude to the integrity of 'character', have led many to hail him as a precursor of the postmodern. But we should avoid prematurely abstracting his work from the time and place that produced it. O'Nolan must also be viewed in historical and geographical context: as a product of post-revolutionary Ireland.

O'Nolan's generation were the heirs to political independence, which was secured for twenty-six counties of Ireland in negotiations between nationalists and the British government in 1921. The formation of the Irish Free State was only the latest chapter in the story of Anglo-Irish relations across several centuries. English invasions of the island date back at least to the twelfth century, but the colonial project was extended and consolidated in the seventeenth and eighteenth centuries. While Protestant settlers were encouraged to colonize the island, Irish Catholics were made second-class citizens in a body of repressive legislation – the Penal Laws – which effectively made eighteenth-century Ireland an apartheid state. From the late eighteenth century on, Ireland would witness a series of movements aiming to re-establish the rights of Catholics and those considering themselves as native Irish. The centuries of English rule also witnessed repeated rebellions against it. The nineteenth century was marked both by constitutional struggles – led most notably by Daniel O'Connell and Charles Stewart Parnell – and by movements seeking violent insurrection against the British presence.

In 1916, a number of political vectors converged in the Easter Rising, the most celebrated and controversial event in modern Irish history. Rebel forces led by the Catholic poet and schoolteacher Patrick Pearse and the socialist James Connolly seized Dublin's General Post Office and declared the Republic of Ireland, but within days they were defeated by British troops. Public disdain for the rebels turned to sympathy when the British made the tactical error of executing their leaders. In a knock-on effect, the Republican party Sinn Féin overtook their more moderate rivals in constitutional nationalism, while Irish rebels led by Michael Collins and Eamon de Valera fought guerrilla battles with British troops, police and intelligence services in the War of Independence (1919–21). The result was negotiation in Downing Street between Lloyd George's government and an Irish delegation led by Collins. A compromise was agreed, in which Irish independence would be granted at a less exalted level than the island-wide Republic sought by the rebels. The result was the Irish Free State, whose most evident shortcoming from a nationalist point of view would seem to be its failure to cover the whole territory of Ireland. Six counties in the north-east remained as part of the United Kingdom, as they do to this day. In 1922, however, the most contentious feature in the Treaty signed by Britain and Ireland was the status of the 'Free' Ireland: it was to remain a Dominion, a member of the Commonwealth, and must swear an oath of fidelity to the Crown. The republican movement split between those in favour of the Treaty and those irreconcilables who branded it a betrayal of the struggle, and from April 1922 to May 1923, civil war between the two factions was the result. The superior military force of the pro-Treaty side won out, and the Irish Free State began to establish itself.

This turbulent political history imprinted itself on every generation in the Ireland of the time. But writers and artists had a particular relation to it. Between around 1880 and 1920, political nationalism had interacted in complex ways with a new surge of cultural nationalism. The various factions of this new movement – often referred to by the overarching term, the 'Irish Revival' – sought to promote Irish culture at the expense of English, with the ultimate aim of laying the ground for political transformation. The Revival took many forms and reached into many modes of 'culture': there were attempts to revive the sports, dancing, folklore which allegedly expressed the nation's soul despite its long experience of British power. Above all, there was an attempt to restore the mass competence in the Irish language which had been decimated by the ascendancy of English. The Gaelic League, founded in 1893, made this chief among its strategies for what its president Douglas Hyde called 'the de-Anglicization of Ireland'.

In reality, the Revival contained conflicting and sometimes antagonistic elements. The starkest distinction was between Catholic and Protestant movements. Many revivalists of Protestant stock saw themselves as heirs to the Anglo-Irish Ascendancy who had formed Ireland's ruling class until the rise of the mass nationalist movement. W. B. Yeats was exemplary of this milieu, in his ethnic affiliations and in his attraction to an exoticized, magical Ireland of fairies, romantic landowning horsemen and wise peasants. These Protestant revivalists were viewed with suspicion, however, by the Catholic 'Irish Ireland' movement, whose leading voices spoke not for the Big House but for the growing nation of Catholic 'shopkeepers' so despised by Yeats. Yet Yeats ran cultural nationalism into a single stream in a retrospective view which proved influential:

> The modern literature of Ireland, and indeed all that stir of thought which prepared for the Anglo-Irish war, began when Parnell fell from power in 1891. A disillusioned and embittered Ireland turned from parliamentary politics; an event was conceived; and the race began, as I think, to be troubled by that event's long gestation.[10]

Yeats implies that the revolution of the years 1916–21 was caused by cultural nationalism – which, given his own prominence in the cultural revival, is virtually to claim authorship of Ireland's independence. In the late poem 'The Statues' he again ponders the political efficacy of art, wondering: 'Did that play of mine send out / Certain men the English shot?'[11] Historians have poured cold water on this kind of speculation, calling into doubt the actual significance of the cultural revival next to more mundane political and economic factors.[12] Yet, whatever the literary revival's political efficacy, it left a legacy in Irish letters that was hard to forget or to transcend. In its exalted claims and its rhetoric of roots, it may be seen as parallel to, rather than direct cause of, the movement for political independence. And it was this dual legacy – of violence and dramatic change in Ireland's politics, and of experiment and high achievement in its literature – which Brian O'Nolan's generation of writers inherited. This was their opportunity and their problem.

Four features of the Free State's culture deserve emphasis.[13] *Self-definition against England* was a powerful factor: like many post-colonial states, independent Ireland devoted much energy to staking out its distinctive national character, in contrast to the former colonial power just across the water. It was emphatically *Catholic*. In 1937 the Taoiseach (prime minister) Eamon de Valera drafted a new Constitution which formalized the relation between church and state, but that relation was already unusually close. The Free State was relatively *socially homogeneous.* The vast majority of the new Ireland were Catholics, and an unusually high proportion of the population was rural: the 1926 Census recorded that 61 per cent lived outside towns and villages.[14] With the Northern counties of Ulster omitted from the state, the new nation was remarkably settled and relatively free of major social and ideological schism. National politics were divided into two main parties, both of which represented the peaceful continuation of one side in the civil war. Fine Gael derived from the pro-Treaty faction, while Fianna Fáil, founded by de Valera in 1926, claimed descent from diehard Republicanism. These differences in nationalist pedigree did not amount to the major ideological differences represented by the party system in most developed countries. Finally, all these factors made for a *culturally conservative* society. Repressive legislation was passed in several areas of cultural life, most notoriously the Censorship of Publications Act 1929. The draconian censorship which this heralded was partly aimed at protecting Ireland from the English popular press – it being understood that immoral publications could not derive from Ireland itself. But the censorship committee also banned the work of many Irish writers. Indeed, to have been banned became a badge of distinction among writers: and Brian O'Nolan actively courted censorship in his late fiction (*NLM* 213–14).

How, more broadly, did O'Nolan fit into this society? He belonged to the very Catholic majority who had seized power, yet had an ambiguous relation to it. From 1929 to 1932 he attended University College, Dublin, an institution founded for Catholics; and here he joined a world of irreverence and mockery, a place where the official pieties of the state were not necessarily respected. A number of O'Nolan's friends and contemporaries – Niall Sheridan, Donagh MacDonagh, Niall Montgomery – were self-styled poets and intellectuals, who relished, and to some extent shared, the brand of irony and humour that O'Nolan was already developing. In different degrees they also shared a scepticism about the literature of the Revival, and about political nationalism itself. But while these shaping forces might be mocked, they were not to be thought away. The Revival had produced a body of work, notably in

11

poetry and drama, that would be hard to equal; and for all the revolution's disappointments, a reversion to British rule was unthinkable. One figure seemed to stand beyond these forces, showing that there had been another way for the Irish artist to go. This was James Joyce.

Joyce's fiction – notably *A Portrait of the Artist as a Young Man* (1916) and *Ulysses* (1922) – had either consummated or liquidated the Revival, or perhaps both. Rich in experiment and audacity, Joyce's works remained obsessed with the Ireland that the man himself had left for the last time in 1912. Until his death in 1941 he lived in a self-imposed European exile which stood as a rebuke to his homeland, and not least to the conservative direction taken by the state after independence. From the standpoint of O'Nolan's generation, a series of factors were constellated in Joyce's writing. There was his Irish Catholic provenance: a former student of UCD, he had already rehearsed much of the biographical subject matter which might have been O'Nolan's own. There was his defiant exile, echoed by his fictional alter-ego Stephen Dedalus's desire to 'fly by the nets' of nationality, language and religion.[15] In his fiction this was reflected by a startling explosion of novelty, a series of shocks both in language and in the subjects portrayed. Joyce's Irish epic had eschewed the Celtic twilight, placing itself instead at the vanguard of contemporary writing. As such, he had joined the republic of letters – had become a major figure in the social formation that would later be called 'international modernism'. Critics have recently sought to demonstrate that Joyce's work nonetheless remained focused on Ireland and its troubled history.[16] But this did not make life any easier for the generation of wits and poets who followed him. The question remained: how to follow *that*?

Perhaps only one member of O'Nolan's generation did so with complete success – though that word was anathema to his art. Samuel Beckett (1906–1989) was of Protestant stock, and thus represented a different social and ethnic experience from Joyce and O'Nolan. Disgusted by the censorious Free State, he followed Joyce into Parisian exile, and wrote a style of prose which owed much to the puns and playfulness of the older writer. Beckett solved this problem of derivativeness by drastic means: he began to write in French, and to translate back from this into a strange new English voice of his own. Beckett thus extended the Joycean line of Euro-Irish modernism, in a uniquely intense and demanding body of work which was to win him the Nobel Prize for Literature in 1969. Brian O'Nolan might be identified as the third man in this trinity. Like Beckett, he had learned from Joyce early on, and developed an intense self-consciousness about words and their multiple meanings. Like both men, he was fundamentally a comic writer, the latest – and one of the greatest – in a tradition of Irish humour.[17] Yet there was to be no Nobel Prize for Brian O'Nolan; and while he himself had been one of the in-augurators of 'Bloomsday' in 1954, he is commemorated by no such international feast day as Joyceans have for their hero. In some sense, he may be considered to have failed: squandering talent, dissatisfied with his own achievement, drinking himself to death at 54. Unlike Joyce and Beckett, O'Nolan never left: he saw out his life in the Dublin suburbs. The Ireland on which his writing fed played its part in its limitations, as well as its brilliant successes. But we are in a position to appreciate, even to reassess, the achievement of Brian O'Nolan. Of Brian O'Nolan? Or of Flann O'Brien? Or – ?

13

1

Yours Sincerely: The Early Years

The parade of masks predated *At Swim-Two-Birds*. By the time his first novel appeared, Brian O'Nolan had produced a wealth of comic writing, which deserves its due alongside his later achievements. The articles he wrote for the UCD magazine *Comhthrom Féinne* (Fair Play) in the early 1930s, and for the short-lived, parodic publication *Blather* in 1934–5, are too numerous to be surveyed comprehensively here. But let us examine a few key examples in which we can watch O'Nolan's humour developing and engaging with its times.

From his earliest writings, O'Nolan is playing with multiple selves, essaying personae. The most significant from the student years is Brother Barnabas, a mysterious cleric more bombastic than monastic. Brother Barnabas foreshadows the later figure of Myles na gCopaleen in his multiplicity: he is less a 'character' than a capacious container for details and possibilities. What will be the multitude of O'Nolan's personae is thus already figured *within* a persona. The casual decentring of the self which his many names will come to suggest is also the condition of the first alternative self he fashions. In December 1933 the magazine printed a retrospective on the life of Brother Barnabas, having interviewed him at his 'rustic bog-farm in the County Meath' (*MBM* 66), and revealed the range of his improbable achievements. In the Vienna of 1912, Barnabas thrashed Kaiser Wilhelm with a dog-whip; he has also burnt down the German Reichstag (having dissolved the Danish Reichstag in 1887), invented mixed dancing, stolen the corsets of the Archduke Nicholas, demanded that pin-money girls be sacked, encountered Sherlock Holmes and Billy Bunter, and 'discovered and hastily re-covered James Joyce' (*MBM* 67–72). In the magazine's next issue he recounts his Russian Jewish provenance and his travels through modernist Europe, which have landed him in Dublin under an assumed Irish name (*MBM* 72–6). Events, places and periods are strung together in absurd juxtapositions: local details and Dublin in-jokes are cheek by jowl with references to world history and famous names. Not for the last time in his career, O'Nolan delights in conjuring an impossible textual space, a range of combinations and juxtapositions which scrape sparks of silliness from each other. The profusion of references to Germany, Russia and Central Europe prompts recollections of the opening stanza of T. S. Eliot's *The Waste Land* (1922):

> Summer surprised us, coming over the Starnbergersee
> With a shower of rain; we stopped in the colonnade,
> And went on in sunlight, into the Hofgarten,
> And drank coffee, and talked for an hour.
> Bin gar keine Russin, stamm' aus Litauen, echt deutsch.[1]

Eliot's poem, like O'Nolan's skits, makes a world out of disparate materials. But the tone is different: Eliot's enigmas are unravelled and ravelled again into the tomfoolery of the untrue history of Brother Barnabas. This is one way of seeing O'Nolan's writing: as a burlesque of modernism, whose materials were nonetheless made possible, laid before him, by the modernists. Elsewhere in *Comhthrom Féinne* he invents a poet, Lionel Prune, whose persona is a belated spoof of W. B. Yeats: 'tall and willowy', his eyes 'vacuous and yearning', the poet 'groan[s] beneath a heavy burthen of jet-black hair long untouched by tonsorial shears' (*MBM* 29). But Prune's verses – produced, in an accelerating comedy of improbability, on his shirt cuffs, his watch, or the back of a dinner plate – more evidently parody Eliot. His piece on the students' Literary and Historical Society (*MBM* 32–3), interrupted by nonsense words ('Wangli Wanglos Wanglorum'), mimics the ancient incantations which punctuate the end of *The Waste Land* and whose ritual authority Eliot became keen to incorporate into his poetry. And Prune's finale – 'Sh-h-h-h!' – is a bathetic allusion to Eliot's closing 'Shantih shantih shantih'.[2] It is characteristic of O'Nolan to have engaged in such parodic demystification of the modernism which was just beginning to establish a canonical niche at this point.[3] It is also rather typical, though, that his parody had already been anticipated by James Joyce, in a private letter of 1925.[4] This summarizes a dilemma which faced O'Nolan as a writer: he existed in a comical, debunking relation to his predecessors, but the most oppressively formidable of those predecessors was himself the most comical and debunking of artists. This ambivalent relation to modernism – debt and doubt entwined – would remain a feature of O'Nolan's work to the end.

In the 1930s O'Nolan peppered his comic writing with references to Germany, Nazi Germany included. The interview which implies that Brother Barnabas burned the German *Reichstag* – which the Nazis did, as a political strategem – is subtitled *'Mein Kampf* ('my struggle': the name of Hitler's political autobiography (*MBM* 66)). In a spoof report from 1932, we read that Brother Barnabas's 'undoubted talents as an election agent had been requisited by Herr Adolf Hitler in the matter of the German presidential elections'. Travelling on a German train, Barnabas gets into an argument with the thinker 'Politicus', and at the Spa of Baden-Baden a boxing match is arranged: Barnabas is 'severely beaten about the head, arms, shoulders, legs and body; Politicus landed thirteen knock-out blows in quick succession' (*MBM* 64).

Should we take this as gleeful imaginary violence against a fascist accomplice? No more than we should take Barnabas's myriad affiliations as a representation of O'Nolan's real views. O'Nolan shows no sign of being swayed by the aura of fascism – unlike such major international figures of the preceding generation as Ezra Pound and Wyndham Lewis. Nor, on the other hand, does his writing demonstrate a strong and articulate hostility to it. One piece in *Blather* is as pointed as it gets: 'Has Hitler Gone Too Far?', asks the magazine in October 1934. The Führer's offence is to have banned *Blather*. This fantasy translates the reality that Hitler has banned the English *Daily Express*, under which name *Blather* here claims to have been 'cunningly circulating':

> Arrangements are in hand by which the next issue of the paper will appear in Germany under the title of the *Daily Mail*. Should a

further decree be issued, *Blather* will have no hesitation in changing the title again to that of *Our Boys*.

And no amount of persecution will prevent us from carefully pointing out the weakness in the social and political fabric of Germany . . . (*MBM* 137)

Fascism joins the cast of ideological characters in O'Nolan's comical theatre: it is fair game for satire, but is teased less frequently than the indigenous authoritarianism of the Irish Free State. Judged in retrospect, O'Nolan's response to fascism appears neither admirable (like Beckett's work with the French Resistance) nor lamentable (like Pound's enthusiasm for Mussolini, or indeed W. B. Yeats's flirtation with homegrown Irish fascism), but somewhat trivial. Triviality, of course, was his speciality, even if in retrospect it seems an inadequate response to European history in this period.

Yet O'Nolan's mockery was not without political bite in the 1930s, when he fixed his satirical attention on the country he knew. A recurrent theme, already, was Irish identity: in particular, the claims of the Literary Revival to have located and fixed the meaning of Irishness. The movement's towering figures, W. B. Yeats and John Millington Synge, are both objects of O'Nolan's mischief. The jibe at Yeats, as we have seen, is dispersed into a more diffuse mockery of modern verse. Synge's art would be a more consistent target for O'Nolan. He snipes at Synge through to *Cruiskeen Lawn*, but never more tellingly than when *Comhthrom Féinne* introduces 'Samuel Hall', the author of *The Bog of Allen*: 'It is a wholesome Irish play, racy of the soil and Samuel Hall, written in the real traditional style, and a masterpiece of characterisation and pregnant dialogue' (*MBM* 40). The play amounts to a couple of pages: space enough for the cult of the West to be laid waste. Its dialogue – 'Shure, wisha, musha, anish now, for goodness sake, what would you be wantin'?' – is Synge-speak ridiculously exaggerated, but still recognizable enough to sting. Most incisive, though, is the opening stage direction:

Scene: The Kitchen in Allen Bogg's hovel in the middle of the Bog of Allen, miles from dry land. The house was built by Gregory B. Bogg, Allen's grandfather. As he could not find sand to build it on, he built it on the Bog. It is a typically Irish household. The floor is flagged with green moss between the cracks. A roaring fire of the best Wigan coal is burning in the hearth. In a corner is a bed with a white sow in it. . . . A bag-pipes are hanging on the wall, but not, unfortunately, so high up that a tall man could not reach them. Over the mantelpiece is a rusty iron pike for use in Insurrections. A rustic and homely smell of fish-and-chips permeates the atmosphere. Over in a corner a cupboard is let into the wall, with a heavy padlock and chain, in which leprechauns are stored. Below on the floor is a primitive rack, made of bog-oak, for torturing leprechauns who will not divulge where the Crock of Gold is hidden. (*MBM* 41)

The text ridicules the fetishization of the west of the country as the real Ireland – 'The Hidden Ireland', as the nationalist critic Daniel Corkery had dubbed it. The Free State had carried over much of the cultural baggage of the Revival: what was essential to Ireland was its countryside, where lingered the indigenous spirituality and integrity unknown to England, or indeed to Unionist Ulster.[5] The bog of Allen is the next best surface to sand, for a builder: a note on the perversity of championing bogs as the ideal home of the people. Nationalism will lay claim to anything that suits its images – moss, for instance, thanks to its being green.[6] At the same time, the hovel is a tableau of national motifs: pig-farming in one corner, Insurrections on the wall, leprechauns in the cupboard. The brisk, deadpan tone forges the space of a flattened, cartoon Ireland. The space, nominally, of a theatre: but an unreal space, a configuration destined never to get beyond the printed page. The theatre of Synge, O'Nolan's lampoon protests, is about as unreal as this: the reverse of the authenticity which is claimed for it. And amidst this critique, other elements bob: Wigan coal, 'rustic and homely' fish and chips. The incongruities are comic in themselves, but the point they seem to make is that Ireland remains wedded to England even in its proud rhetoric of disassociation. The polemic, such as it is, might seem contradictory: can O'Nolan be laughing at Irish exceptionalism *and* scorning the country's continuing relations with the British? But what the passage appears to nail is the embarrassing contradiction between the two.

The state of Ireland was also the prime theme carnivalized by *Blather*, the magazine that O'Nolan produced with his brother

Ciarán and Niall Sheridan in the mid-1930s. *Blather*, like O'Nolan's other projects, had diverse sources. It intervened in a local market dominated by *Dublin Opinion*, a rival often guyed in the pages of *Blather*. Its tone appears to draw on a contemporary English comic publication, *Razzle* – albeit with a distinctively Irish content replacing that of the London magazine, and with political satire far outweighing *Razzle*'s barrage of sexual innunendo. At the same time, *Blather* can productively be read as an ironic echo of those European avant-garde groups – Futurism, Dada and Surrealism – in which the individual artist was also a member of the collaborative group. Rather than the single-authored opus, the energies of the avant-gardes tended to run into joint productions – magazines and manifestos – before bubbling over or breaking up. Many theorists of twentieth-century art have followed the German critic Peter Bürger in viewing avant-garde practice as open, experimental, even chaotic, and as aiming to integrate art and life in estranging new ways.[7] As what Anne Clissmann dubs an 'anti-magazine' (*FOB* 57), *Blather* offers a new, satirical version of this approach to art. *Blather* sets itself against the conventions of magazine publishing, not by a chaos of unreadability but through deadly accurate parody. A short-lived parasite on the back of the existing media, *Blather* does not so much set its face against convention as perform gurning impressions of it. Cliché and norm are mined, and left exploded and exposed.

To make such claims for *Blather* is to pre-empt the magazine's own rhetoric, which can be relied on to speak for itself:

> Blather is here.
>   As we advance to make our bow, you will look in vain for signs of servility or for any evidence of a slavish desire to please. We are an arrogant and a depraved body of men. We are as proud as bantams and as vain as peacocks. *Blather* doesn't care.
>   . . . .
>   *Blather* has no principles, no honour, no shame. Our objects are the fostering of graft and corruption in public life, the furthering of cant and hypocrisy, the encouragement of humbug and hysteria, the glorification of greed and gombeenism.   (*MBM* 96–7)

This is from the first editorial, which toys with different registers and aims at a variety of effects. The most basic contradiction in the magazine's rhetoric, as John Wyse Jackson notes, is between arrogance and abnegation: '*Blather* emphasizes its own vast importance at the same time as it announces that it is just a poor amateur affair, not worth the paper it besmirches' (*MBM* 96). What the two tones share is hyperbole. Whether flexing imaginary muscles or dismissing itself, the magazine must go to extremes. It is in this cultivation of extremity that *Blather* aims to estrange the public world upon which it is thrust: only by constant exaggeration can that world be outstripped and absurdized. In this much the project resembles its predecessors in the continental avant-gardes, for which overstatement had been norm and necessity. The incorrigibly overheated assertions of *Blather* are a belated Dublin rendition of this idiom.

Yet they are also a ceaseless comic performance. *Blather* borrows the extremity and self-promotion of the avant-garde, but can't take it seriously: its own rhetoric is as much the object of laughter as any of the features of Irish life it guys. The avant-gardes had included strong comical and parodic aspects themselves, specializing in the grotesque and absurd: but these had usually been in the service, or at least the company, of serious polemics on art and politics. In *Blather*, the challenge is to find anything serious at all. The magazine undercuts itself at every step, correctly predicting its own demise in a bar chart which shows its projected sales monthly figures shrinking to invisibility:

> Those of our readers who are lucky enough to be working in laboratories can try the diagram under the microscope. If there is no result, they can try playing the page on the gramophone, using, if at all possible, a fibre needle. If there is no result, they can try putting it under the Hoover. If there is still no result, they have one last resort – blue litmus paper. If there is no chemical reaction, they can run along and buy sweeties, as people who spend their time on fool games like that deserve a few sweeties for their pains. What do *you* say?   (*MBM* 124)

Flann O'Brien will return to the mind-bending qualities of invisible things in *The Third Policeman*. What we can note here is what's done with the self-deprecating starting point. It is extended into a kind of list, which inanely repeats ('If there is no result') through a series of physical incongruities ('try playing the page on the gramophone'), before being thrown up in the air ('run along and buy sweeties') and dismissed ('fool games', the magazine now says of its own recommendations). Finally *Blather* turns to the reader: 'What do *you* say?' is a characteristic gesture, disarmingly direct, spoof-solemn as it genuflects to (or does it patronize?) the consumer. The paper regularly claims to have intimate knowledge of its reader:

> 'Not only that', you will write to us and say, 'but my grand piano is gone as well'.
> But we know you.
> You never had a grand piano.   (*MBM* 122)

The difficulty in describing *Blather* is keeping up: its tone slides from mode to mode with mercurial ease, parodying sundry targets, then collapsing in on itself. The reader is addressed with wide-eyed mock politeness ('The credit is yours as well as ours. Are you glad?', *MBM* 122) in the midst of bogus special offers and fake competitions. These are trails that lead nowhere: *Blather* sets up the forms and functions of a modern magazine, but has no intention of seeing them through. The magazine genre is a surface on which to perform travesty and wit: behind it there is only O'Nolan's band of mockers. In this sense *Blather* functions like a mask, a two-dimensional disguise. Though *Blather* only lasts from August to January, O'Nolan will not be done with disguises in a hurry.

Comedy in *Blather*, as in much of O'Nolan's career, goes all the way down. We can rarely say, with this writer, that laughter is merely a tool in the service of some more solemn goal: for anything as solemn as all that will itself be laughed at soon enough. But the satire of *Blather* nonetheless exists in relation to the real world, the serious society against which its lunatic humour stands out. Irish party politics repeatedly provide its targets. The first editorial states that the magazine's aim is to 'injure and wreck the existing political parties', by means of 'distortion, misrepresentation and long-distance lying'. Indeed, 'Much in the way of corruption has already been done. We have de Valera and the entire Fianna Fáil Cabinet in our pocket; we have O'Duffy in a sack' – the list goes on (*MBM* 97). The tone strikes directly at the role of vested interests in Irish politics, to which Myles na gCopaleen would repeatedly return. But more broadly, what *Blather* offers is a political fantasy: a looking-glass land in which the pieties of politics are reconfigured to absurd effect. This is nowhere more vivid than in the crude photo-montages in which the head of Eamon de Valera is superimposed on the body of a long-jumper (*MBM* 128) or a baby (*MBM* 140), while his name is attached to a figure wearing a kettle on its head (*MBM* 141). Meanwhile, a portrait photograph of the prime minister is mislabelled 'Mr Silas P. Hotchkiss. President of the Clanbrassil Street Brass Fender Founders and Tinsmiths' Protection Association, Inc' (*MBM* 140). Knockabout stuff: but the knockabout is the starker for taking as its subject the man who would extend his piety to the nation in the Constitution of 1937, and whose refusal to negotiate the Treaty of 1921 had been excused on the grounds that – as president of the putative Republic – he was not a politician but a symbol.[8] In other words, the silliness of *Blather* appears in greater relief – and may have *been* a greater relief – the more solemn its subject matter. *Blather* – like *Cruiskeen Lawn* later on – manages to dream up an alternative Ireland, a ludic place which is the distorted mirror of the Free State and its post-colonial constraints. Along the way it also belittles the assertions of the actual Ireland, as in its quixotic campaign on behalf of a small town on the Meath coast:

The present agitation for proper Atlantic ports at Galway, Killybegs and elsewhere, has in no small measure displeased *Blather*. Why? The reason is very simple. The pre-eminent claims of Bettystown have been passed over, and it is the sheerest folly on the part of those concerned to imagine that *Blather* is going to stand for it.

Ever since the good people of Bettystown bade The O'Blather a hearty *céad míle fáilte* when he went there to recuperate after his illness in 1924, *Blather* has had its eye on Bettystown. Only for five minutes was the *Blather* eye taken off Bettystown in those ten long years, and that was for two minutes in 1932, when the eye was moved up eight miles to watch the first train crossing the reconstructed viaduct over the Boyne and Drogheda. Nothing happened; the structure held, and the eye was immediately refixed on Bettystown. (*MBM* 106)

The O'Blather – fabled proprietor of the magazine – offers a speech in praise of the place, including the promise to 'build and adorn Bettystown until it becomes the fairest and the brightest gem in the diadem of Eire'. 'Nor', adds *Blather*,

> are the claims of the town in anywise extravagant. Ten years ago their demands were modest: 'Parity with Jerrettspass!' was the simple rallying-cry of the good townspeople. It was only after a hard and bitter fight that this was conceded. . . . Today Bettystown, marching with the times and eager to seize the opportunities opened up by the progress of modern life, asks in a voice that is dispassionate, free alike from the thick bluff of the bully and the fawning pleading of the cringer, that it be provided an Atlantic deep-water harbour. (*MBM* 107)

The exalted claims for the naval potential of Bettystown rebound on to those places whose nautical claims really were being exalted. They sound just as strategically vital as Bettystown: and this at a time when the military use of ports was still a sensitive issue between British and Irish governments. It was not until 1938 that de Valera, in negotiation with Neville Chamberlain, regained six ports which had been pledged to provide Britain with support in time of war. Neutrality, de Valera told his supporters, was not a real possibility until Ireland had regained possession of these.[9] Yet when World War Two broke out, Joseph Lee bluntly notes, 'For practical purposes, Ireland had neither an air force nor a navy'.[10] *Blather* suggests that Ireland's proud strides towards securing its sovereignty are equivalent to the vital task of developing Bettystown harbour. At points like this, its textual carnival is also a political insult – not that *Blather* would never lower itself to the discursive standards set by other, *serious* commentators.

Blather was a kind of collective façade, and it was purportedly backed by another fiction: the O'Blather, aged statesman and proprietor. But in the mid-1930s O'Nolan had hardly begun to assemble his gallery of guises. 'Flann O'Brien', we have seen, was born an adult in 1939. Yet whoever the Flann O'Brien of *At Swim-Two-Birds* was, he had an odd alternate life in the *Irish Times* of 1940. Here, on two occasions, Brian O'Nolan and his friends developed spurious, lengthy debate on the letters pages. In June 1940, a controversy was manufactured out of an innocent reader's letter requesting that the Dublin public should support its theatre. O'Nolan wrote to the paper as 'F. O'Brien, Dublin', and a series of other strange aliases followed this one into the discussion. The controversy spiralled into a surreal series of ridiculous claims about great literary figures, whom the various correspondents claimed to have known personally. F. O'Brien, Lir O'Connor, Whit Cassidy and others outbid and outdid each other in deliberately absurd assertions about the hair of Henrik Ibsen or the sex of Joseph ('Josephine') Conrad. The controversy lasted over a fortnight, and exactly a month after its end a new one was generated, this time around a book review by the poet Patrick Kavanagh. Contributors included H.P., Whit Cassidy, Paul Desmond, Luna O'Connor, 'F.L.J', N. S. Harvey, Judy Clifford, Jno. O'Ruddy, Hilda Upshott, The O'Madan, 'South American Joe', 'Lanna Avvia', 'Na2 Co3', and F. McEwe Obarn – not to mention the mysterious Oscar Love, a shadowy figure whose name appears to gesture back at the teasing personae of Wilde. Through the first summer of the Second World War, an unusual amount of space was given over to this farcical activity.

Like *Blather*, the controversies were a joint production. It is difficult to ascertain which letters were written by O'Nolan and which by his friends – though, as John Wyse Jackson points out, the style of humour 'was his own, or he made it his own' (*MBM* 10). The reader of one of the controversies is faced with a mysterious body of writing, whose peculiar character deserves some reflection. In one sense it is inherently a thing of fragments, a chance collection of bits to be placed in chronological sequence. Its authors are certainly multiple, though we cannot be sure how multiple. It has no predetermined order, no destination inscribed in it from the start: it is a text whose end its first author cannot foresee. At the same time, the controversy possesses a kind of continuity: the comic spirit that runs through the whole is a signal asking not only to be received and interpreted correctly, but to be appropriated and redirected. The debate tacitly asks those who get it to join in and extend it: to pick up the tone is to enlist in a restricted club. A kind of unitary work – though one without a central narrative – is fashioned: but this is done by accident. Planned accident: the chancy nature of the letters column, which might always attract another uninvited author, is taken into account, chosen as the very basis of the enterprise. The fake controversy is built on the vagaries of the public textual space offered by the newspaper: it acknowledges and invites the irruption of contingency and surprise.

A number of the central features of O'Nolan's work are clearly visible here, as they had been in *Blather*. We may note the following. Comedy is the genre of choice – a comedy pushing towards absurdity and the ridiculous. Authorship is not single or clear, but scattered among a series of names. The work is a collation of fragments, disjointed almost by design. It is open to chance and contingency. It takes place in public – and not in a book, but in the workaday reams of the daily press. Yet it is also somewhat esoteric: its tone must be decoded by the able. It forms a sort of secret message in plain view: the reading matter, perhaps, of a coterie with the right references.

Patrick Kavanagh, bringing the second controversy to a close, thought that he had detected another, more telling feature. In the review that had started the second controversy, he recalled, he had written of 'the empty virtuosity of artists who are expert in saying nothing. Ploughmen without land. . . . if ever a critic was proved right, all round, by his critics it happened this time' (*MBM* 225). Kavanagh believes that he has seen through to the vacant heart of the epistolary satirists:

> It is to be feared that the diletanttish disciples of Joyce and Eliot are no more a credit to their masters than are the followers of Lord Baden-Powell and Margaret Mitchell [the Boy Scouts and *Gone With The Wind* had featured in the controversy]. I am referring chiefly to the undergraduate-magazine writers who reached the heights of epic literature in a balloon filled with verbal gas. . . .
>
> As I write these words a feeling of deep pity comes over me – the pity that is awakened by the contortions of a clown's funny face. . . . There is tragedy here, and I for one, am shy to bring these literary scouts and touts to a raw awareness of their tragedy. Too soon they will know the misery of literary men without themes, poets without burdens, ploughmen without land.   (*MBM* 225)

Kavanagh seizes the tone of the conversation, abruptly rein-stating the voice of regretful sincerity in the teeth of the many layers of irony which have preceded this contribution. His admonition is oddly rich in implication, and is worth mulling over.

'Undergraduate-magazine writers': given that they had graduated some eight years previously, this is less a description than a condemnation. The correspondents, in Kavanagh's eyes, are young wits, callow, untested souls. His central charge is emptiness: O'Nolan can generate verbiage from nothing, spin the most elaborate of forms around the most minimal content. The terms of Kavanagh's description suggest an opposition between earth and air: the land that the honest literary ploughman needs, and the air into which the ballooning 'gas-man' sails. This looks like a version of the opposition between the Irish Revival and Joyce: on one hand localism, peasantry, the rural; on the other, the Dedalian flight beyond nets and constraints, into the airspace of modernity. In this sense, O'Nolan's faction carries the sign of the future, the literary attitude which will last into the rootless days of the later twentieth century: Kavanagh's is a naïve rhetoric of earth. Still, there is something more precise at stake in Kavanagh's critique: for he is drawing a distinction between the generation of Joyce and that of O'Nolan, the high modernist and the man who comes after. The latter figure is the 'dilettante', left – *unlike* his modernist heroes – with nothing to say. The 'tragedy' Kavanagh posits is the predicament of the writer in this time and place, faced with the complex realities of political independence rather than the impending dream of the Republic; the writer, Anthony Cronin adds, whose subject matter has been given its definitive treatment by Joyce (*NLM* ix). Kavanagh's ultimate implication is that O'Nolan's writing is already showing its decadence, its essential superfluity – its essential *inessentiality*. He warns the reader, at the start of O'Nolan's literary career, to watch for the tears of the clown.

2

Odd Numbers:
At Swim-Two-Birds

'One beginning and one ending for a book was a thing I did not agree with', the narrator of *At Swim-Two-Birds* tells us in its first paragraph: 'A good book may have three openings entirely dissimilar and inter-related only in the prescience of the author, or for that matter one hundred times as many endings' (*AS* 9). True to his word, the narrator then offers us '*Examples of three separate openings*' before we get past the first page. The three proffered paragraphs do not narrate the same events in different ways, or offer different routes into what is evidently a single story. They are radically different from each other, describing characters from different milieux or narrative conventions: an Irish folk devil; a contemporary Dubliner who has just been born at the age of twenty-five; the legendary hero Finn MacCool. From the start, *At Swim-Two-Birds* is a book which refuses to be one book: which wants to be many. The novel is founded on multiplicity, on the proliferation of stories and worlds. John Garvin, O'Nolan's mentor in the Civil Service, supplied a Greek epigraph – 'All things yield each other place' – which emphasizes the autonomy and multiplicity of the book's components. In the event, these three narratives will meet up and become part of a single situation. But the very absurdity of this world – in which Finn MacCool and the Pooka MacPhellimey walk through a contemporary Ireland populated by cowboys, talking cows, and people who have been created from thin air – will undermine its unity. A book composed of such heterogeneous material will not settle into plausibility: in bringing these incompatible subjects together, it will shred the notion of literary realism.

The unity of these characters and motifs is impossible: but in a sense the novel is toying with impossibility from the start. What can it mean to want one book to contain several; or for a book to begin three times? Wouldn't the first beginning be the beginning? Or if the three beginnings are separate enough not to claim numerical priority over each other, how can they be the beginnings to one book, rather than three separate ones? And can a book legitimately end more times than it begins? There may be no definitive answers to these questions, outside a catechism of the anti-novel. In *At Swim-Two-Birds*, the paradox of the three beginnings is already gently ironized by the fact that *this* book (the one by 'Flann O'Brien') has already begun, with a paragraph starting, 'Having placed in my mouth sufficient bread for three minutes' chewing, I withdrew my powers of sensual perception and retired into the privacy of my mind . . .' (*AS* 9). Of course it has already begun: how else could we have been told about the theory of multiple beginnings, before the beginnings started? Before even that first paragraph, in fact, *At Swim-Two-Birds* begins, uncontroversially enough,

CHAPTER I.   (*AS* 9)

This is a fact worth mentioning, for once, because there is no CHAPTER II in the subsequent 200 pages. It feels like an oversight, or a convention (break your book into chapters) adopted but botched.[1] More strikingly, this is to be a book with three beginnings (and, as it happens, three endings) but only one chapter: an inversion on every front, a structure gone awry, a novel with a difference – with nothing but difference.

Yet it is also a story-book: it seeks to unfold not just one tale, but as many as possible, even if – especially if – that sets it askew to the way novels are supposed to work. *At Swim-Two-Birds* is *about* story, but it also *has* a story, stories plural. It is impossible to describe the novel's complex workings without also giving an account of what it works upon: we can't intelligibly talk about its forms without listing its contents. Yet these two aspects interfere with each other in the other

28

direction too. It is difficult to describe 'what happens' without also discussing *how* it happens, as a textual event. To recount the story is always to be pulled into a discussion of storytelling: to narrate the events of this novel is inexorably to be sidetracked into an analysis of narrative process. This inextricability of form and content is not just a difficulty for the critic, but a central fact about the book. Part of the meaning of *At Swim* is its refusal to behave like an ordinary novel: much of its distinctiveness resides in its resistance to being 'translated' into simpler terms. To recount the plot of a novel is always to lose something (that is, the actual texture and experience of the novel): but to do this with *At Swim* is to lose almost everything, insofar as 'plot' here is a whim, an occasion. Insofar, that is – and here we approach one definition of the book's distinctiveness – as plot is a vehicle for narrative process, rather than the other way around.

Still – about that story. *At Swim-Two-Birds* is a novel in which a man writes a novel in which another man writes a novel, whose characters take over the writing of the novel and take revenge upon their author. One thing that even this summary tells us is that *At Swim-Two-Birds* is a book of books, a novel whose conceit is that it contains other novels, each folded inside the last. The images of Chinese boxes or Russian dolls, each smaller than its predecessor, come readily to hand. Like Policeman MacCruiskeen's boxes in *The Third Policeman* (*TP* 72–6), stories nestle within other stories, and each narrative layer opens successively on to the next in a *mise en abyme* effect. Yet even this description makes the book sound less complex and troublesome than it really is, for *At Swim* refuses to maintain a straightforward, easily grasped relation between narrative levels. It cuts frequently back and forth between the 'frame' story and the fictional worlds that lie within it; it multiplies and leaves uncertain the number of fictional worlds which coexist on a given level; it invents bizarre new rules for the relations between (fictional) author, text and characters, then abruptly alters them, pulling the rug out from under the reader at the last.

Let us examine more slowly the novel's different levels of narration, and the peculiar fictional logic that results. My assumption in this account is that there are three different narrative layers, which for the convenience of the reader I shall dub A, B and C. The man who, before writing this novel, had invented a means for translating Gaelic into algebra (*MBM* 56–61) might have understood.

The primary narrative (A) is delivered in ten 'Biographical Reminiscences' by a student in his final year at University College, Dublin, where O'Nolan had spent the first half of the 1930s. This first–person voice of this nameless figure is effectively the frame for everything else in the book. (Sue Asbee has pointed out that the anonymity of the narrator is itself a wilfully awkward aspect of the book: any account of the story must labour clumsily with the non-name 'the narrator'.[2] Here I shall call him 'the student', in order to make it easier to discuss the novel's multiple voices.) The student lives with his uncle, a Guinness clerk who is sceptical of his nephew's dedication to study. This suspicion appears justified, as much of the student's narrative shows him drinking and talking with friends from UCD. Most significant of all are his 'spare-time literary activities' (*AS* 9): he is writing a novel, which he spends much of *At Swim* expounding and discussing. Despite all this, the story ends with the student having passed his exams, and being congratulated with unusual warmth by the uncle.

These events might make the basis of an engaging novel if it were fully developed. We can imagine a radically different book which would detail the travails of the parentless student, struggling against the yoke of the uncle and the pieties of the older generation, developing aesthetic theories and literary ideas with his contemporaries, and finally triumphing academically against all expectations. Importantly, though, Flann O'Brien did *not* write that imagined book. The story of the student refuses to be a generic memoir of youth in two major ways: stylistic and structural. We can continue the pursuit of the latter – the extraordinary 'story-teller's book-web' (*AS* 19) that *At Swim* represents – in a moment. But we should first note the stylistic strangeness offered even by the primary narrative.

The dialogue spoken in these scenes is colloquially colourful, peppered with Hiberno-English locutions: 'Tell me this, do you ever open a book at all?' (*AS* 10); 'By God you're the bloody queer man' (*AS* 23); 'Well, dear knows it must be a great book altogether that can cost five shillings' (*AS* 33). This only emphasizes further the peculiar impersonality of the student's own narrative voice. At best he is formal: 'I perused a number of public notices attached to the wall and then made my way without offence to the back of the College, where there was another old ruined College containing an apartment known as the Gentlemen's Smokeroom. This room was usually occupied by card-players, hooligans and rough persons' (*AS* 34). This has the care of a policeman reading from his notebook. Simple facts are described with as elaborate a precision as possible: 'Innumerable persons with whom I had conversed had represented to me that spirituous liquors and intoxicants generally had an adverse effect on the senses and the body and that those who became addicted to stimulants in youth were unhappy throughout their lives and met with death at the end by a drunkard's fall . . .' (*AS* 21). The formality can also shade into something else: 'The College is outwardly a rectangular plain building with a fine porch where the midday sun pours down in summer from the Donnybrook direction, heating the steps for the comfort of the students' (*AS* 33). The detachment with which the student describes the world has estranged it: does the sun – from the Donnybrook direction, of all stellar sources – really heat the steps for the benefit of the students? An equivalent detachment affects the student's reference to the body: 'Through the two apertures of my eyes I gazed out in a hostile manner' (*AS* 34), he writes, as though the eyes are instruments to be deployed – and as though the manner, for that matter, can be switched on or off at will.

This is a purposely cold prose, meticulously drained of abbreviation and colloquialism. The Dublin dialect which fills the student's social world is utterly absent from his own narration: 'familiarity' – as opposed to formality – has been banned, and with it the world is made unfamiliar. As Anthony Cronin remarks, the narrator seems to be writing English as a dead language (*NLM* 106). A kind of depersonalization, Cronin adds, takes place. In a sense this squares with O'Nolan's general penchant for persona and mask: in writing a first-person narrator who attends his own alma mater, he deliberately makes it difficult for us to identify with the student, or to see the figure as a warmly nostalgic version of himself. The style thus refuses the seductions of the memoir, almost as Beckett's flip into French refused him what he considered the too easily won warmth of Hiberno-English.

The style gets even stranger than that. It regularly interrupts itself with a kind of headline, which signals a factual digression:

> We had three drinks in all in respect of each of which Brinsley paid a sixpence without regret.
> *The ultimate emptors*: Meath County Council, rural rating authority. (*AS* 47)

Or in a more extended instance whose variations become a motif through the novel,

> *Description of my uncle*: Red-faced, bead-eyed, ball-bellied. Fleshy about the shoulders with long swinging arms giving ape-like effect to gait. Large moustache. Holder of Guinness clerkship the third class. (*AS* 10)

The form here is the list rather than the statement: the drive to efficiency has displaced the concern for grammar. This paragraph represents a rationalization of information, a streamlining of the narrative to its most rudimentary function: the disclosure of facts. At moments like these, it is as though the novelistic apparatus has been switched off and all that is left running is a kind of database, unprocessed by the niceties of storytelling.

Even if *At Swim* never got out of UCD, then, it would be an odd, disorienting book by virtue of its style. Odder still, though, is the book's departure from this mode. It is in its proliferation of narratives that *At Swim* decisively leaves behind the consolations of the memoir, the trajectory of the *Bildungsroman*. The student offers the frame-story, but we cannot necessarily say that his fate is at the centre of the novel. On the contrary, we might say, the 'frame' is just where one would expect it to be: on the edge, a mere structure for holding something else in place. What is certain is that there are more layers of narrative than this first one alone.

Those other layers, paradoxically, are contained within the first. The student is writing a novel (B) about an author named

Dermot Trellis, who is in turn writing a book of his own (C). Trellis's work is to have a moral purpose, albeit deviously executed, as the student explains:

> Trellis . . . is writing a book on sin and the wages attaching thereto. He is a philosopher and a moralist. He is appalled by the spate of sexual and other crimes recorded in recent times in the newspapers. . . . He realizes that purely a moralizing tract would not reach the public. Therefore he is putting plenty of smut into his book. (*AS* 35)

Trellis's book is to function as literary aversion therapy: the characters and deeds it depicts will be so depraved as to repel its readers into righteousness.

We are therefore dealing, in effect, with three different texts: the story of the student (A), the novel being written by him (B), and the novel being written by Trellis (C). As we reach this third level, things become more complicated. Within the world of the student's novel (B), fiction moves in mysterious ways. 'Characters' have a physical existence: 'authors' cannot simply write them into existence, but must employ them, picking them up from other books and paying for their presence. A literary character is not a textual construct whose every word and gesture is at the command of their author, but a hired hand, brought in to populate or enliven a story. The alternative to this model is, if anything, even more bizarre: 'aesthoautogamy', in which characters can be created from thin air, 'from an operation involving neither fertilization nor conception' (*AS* 40). Lacking a suitably bad man to play his villain, Trellis must conceive of John Furriskey himself, as a spoof newspaper extract reports: 'Stated to be doing "very nicely", the new arrival is about five feet eight inches in height, well built, dark, and clean-shaven. The eyes are blue and the teeth well-formed and good, though stained somewhat by tobacco . . .' (*AS* 40).

Whether manufactured or hired, the characters who are to populate Trellis's novel are like cinematic or dramatic actors: to some extent under the instructions of the author, but always liable to protest at their treatment or to improvise a narrative of their own. As the student puts it in an explanation of his own literary theory,

Each [character] should be allowed a private life, self-determina-
tion and a decent standard of living. This would make for
self-respect, contentment and better service. . . . Characters should
be interchangeable as between one book and another. The entire
corpus of existing literature should be regarded as a limbo from
which discerning authors could draw their characters as required,
creating only when they failed to find a suitable existing puppet.
The modern novel should be largely a work of reference. (*AS* 25)

That last line says much about O'Brien's fiction, and it will
recur in the course of this book. But the whole passage
exemplifies *At Swim*'s comic interrogation of the norms of
fiction. For instance, the conceit of aestho-autogamy, as Anne
Clissmann has noted, is a deliberate *reductio ad absurdum* of the
idea of 'creating a character' (*FOB* 90). We can observe here a
central tendency in Brian O'Nolan's humour, which runs from
Comhthrom Féinne to *Cruiskeen Lawn*: the literalization of what
was metaphorical. The characteristic result of this device is a
queer new scenario which seems radically askew from the
world as we know it, yet which has its own kind of coherence,
thanks to the rigour of the literalization. In the case of *At Swim*,
the effect is an estrangement of our ideas of fiction, character
and authorship. Comedy and critique are hand in hand, as
Anthony West observed in 1939: 'It is inspired nonsense that
makes one laugh a great deal; it carries on another level a good
deal of witty and intelligent criticism of the structure of novel
that gives one pleasure of another sort'.[3] Anne Clissmann has
pointed out (*FOB* 90–91) the way in which O'Brien's japes here
reflect upon the conventions of realist fiction – as influentially
sketched, for instance, by E. M. Forster in *Aspects of the Novel*
(1927). It is as though Flann O'Brien has taken those conventions at their word, and written the novel that they logically
imply but have never hitherto produced. To that extent, the
flagrant fantasies of *At Swim-Two-Birds* have their roots in an
immanent critique of the realist novel: by taking that form's
terms literally, it turns it into a textual circus which is the very
opposite of literary realism.

The oddity is heightened by the range of characters involved
in Trellis's book. Some belong, unproblematically enough, to
contemporary Dublin: prominent among them are 'plain men'
John Furriskey, Paul Shanahan and Antony Lamont (*AS* 61).[4]

But the range of characters involved is far wider than this. The motif of characters for hire is best exemplified by a team of cowboys, rustled by Trellis from the works of a rival author, William Tracy. Their activities open out onto a whole world of literary employment, as in this description of their rival: 'Red Kiersay, you understand, was working for another man by the name of Henderson that was writing another book about cattle-dealing and jobbing and shipping bullocks to Liverpool' (*AS* 54). The Dublin cowboys already take us away from plausible contemporary reality, into a world of comic disloca-tion. But stranger creatures than they are involved. Trellis has also created the Pooka Fergus MacPhellimey, 'A species of human Irish devil endowed with magical powers' (*AS* 61), a character who makes his first full appearance halfway through *At Swim*, when he is approached by a Good Fairy (*AS* 103). Trellis has also hired Finn MacCool, a figure from Irish legend, to be Peggy's guardian; and it is he whose lumbering oral narratives introduce another ancient Gaelic figure, mad King Sweeny, into the text. Sweeny initially appears to be a function of Finn MacCool's recitals. But eventually he is discovered injured in a forest by the other characters (*AS* 125): he has, in effect, fallen from one textual level on to another.

The relation between textual levels proves unstable in another sense too. A central event in the student's manuscript is the birth of Trellis's illegitimate son, Orlick – who arrives, perhaps unsurprisingly in this book, as a 'stocky young man' in 'dark well-cut clothing', his first words a piece of oratorical eloquence (*AS* 145–6). The other characters – notably the 'plain men' Furriskey, Shanahan and Lamont – are by now chafing under Trellis's regime, and seek to punish him for their poor treatment. Having drugged Trellis into sleep, they thus per-suade Orlick – who has inherited Trellis's literary gifts – to take up the author's pen and seize command of his father's story. He readily accepts, as the student records in the course of another synopsis:

> Smouldering with resentment at the stigma of his own bastardy, the dishonour and death of his mother, and incited by the subversive teachings of the Pooka, he agrees. He comes one evening to his lodging where the rest of his friends are gathered

and a start is made on the manuscript in the presence of the interested parties. Now read on.   (*AS* 164)

What follows is Orlick's manuscript: a radical departure in which we see the author, Trellis, turned into a character in someone else's story. This development throws the structure of *At Swim* into reverse. Until now the conceit has been that one character (A) writes about another (B), who writes about another (C): each narrator having the authority befitting an author. But Orlick's narrative exploits the conditions that pertain within the student's novel: the ontological plane which Trellis and his minions share. If characters are as real as their author, then why should they not be able to script his activities, rather than the other way around? The jest, again, relates to everyday metaphors about storytelling: this time what is literalized is the idea that characters can 'take over the story', that a novel has 'got out of hand'.

Yet the process that now occurs is anything but everyday: it requires us to shift our conception of how writing works. What follows is the most *dynamic* depiction of writing that *At Swim-Two-Birds* has to offer. 'Tuesday had come down through Dundrum and Foster Avenue', Orlick begins, 'brine-fresh from sea-travel, a corn-yellow sun-drench that called forth the bees at an incustomary hour to their day of bumbling' (*AS* 164–5). This ornate and circumlocutory prose persists for two pages describing Trellis's awakening, until the story is abruptly interrupted:

> I beg your pardon, Sir, said Shanahan, but this is a bit too high up for us. This delay, I mean to say. The fancy stuff, couldn't you leave it out or make it short, Sir? Couldn't you give him a dose of something, give him a varicose vein in the bloody heart and get him out of that bed?   (*AS* 166–7)

We are thus brought back from the third narrative level (C) to the second (B): and the next forty pages or so are spent cutting between these two. In one sense we have simply seen authorial power change hands – as if, back in contemporary Dublin (A), the narrator's uncle had taken over the writing of Trellis and company (B). But the situation is more mind-bending than that: for it appears that what Orlick writes as 'fiction' actually happens to Trellis. The characters' glee at seeing him mauled by the Pooka and hauled before a judge and jury is not an imaginary compensation for his treatment of them: it is an actual revenge, which is intended to lead to his physical destruction. Narrative has become a weapon, not just meta-phorically – a means, say, of damaging another's reputation – but literally.[5] To narrate Trellis's bruising and demise is to accomplish it: to determine an action on level C is to accomplish it on level B too. To return to the earlier theatrical metaphor: it's as though Orlick and friends have become directors who can order Trellis to perform dangerous stunts, and he is powerless to refuse. For he has now become 'just a character in a novel', in precisely the way that Furriskey, Shanahan and the others managed to avoid.

Towards the end of the novel, then, narrative levels seem to implode into one another: the demarcation between them becomes hard to locate. In a final irony, though, Trellis escapes his scripted fate, through a loophole in the book's weird laws. The student has already brought his own narrative (A) to an end, when we encounter the 'Conclusion of the Book, penultimate' (AS 215). Teresa, Trellis's maidservant, casually makes a fire with 'several sheets of writing which were littered here and there about the floor':

> By a curious coincidence as a matter of fact strange to say it happened that these same pages were those of the master's novel, the pages which made and sustained the existence of Furriskey and his true friends. Now they were blazing, curling and twisting and turning black, straining uneasily in the draught and then taking flight as if to heaven through the chimney. (AS 215–6)

Immediately, a bedraggled Trellis appears outside the front door. The implication is clear: in destroying written descrip-tions of the characters, Teresa destroys them altogether. It has seemed until now that characters have a certain autonomy. Suddenly, they appear to be paper tigers, as fragile as the sheets they're written on: less than a pack of cards. The narrative of *At Swim* has been stripped from three levels to two: both of which, as a sickly Trellis retires to bed again, are now ended.

But *At Swim-Two-Birds* is not quite over. 'Stupidity', wrote Gustave Flaubert, 'is the need for conclusions'.[6] By those lights, this is either a book of rare obtuseness – one whose desire to conclude is so strong that it does it three times over – or a work of unusual intelligence, which repeatedly seeks to postpone its last word. The 'Conclusion of the book, ultimate' is a brief, disturbing dance through a jumble of ideas and motifs. In the course of an apparently aimless discourse on madness, Trellis and Sweeny momentarily reappear, along with mysterious declarations like that with which the passage begins: 'Evil is even, truth is an odd number and death is a full stop' (AS 216). There are certainly ways of connecting this long last paragraph with the novel that precedes it (and the connections were clearer in an earlier draft (MBM 183–5)); but in structural terms it is important to note that we have at last, in effect, fallen out of the book. The student, Dermot and Orlick Trellis, Finn MacCool – all the layered narrators of At Swim-Two-Birds have left the stage, and what is left running at the end is a voice without identifiable origin, counting down to an ending obsessed with numbers. The book began by announcing the desirability of beginning a book three times: as it ends for the third time, it recounts

> the case of the poor German who was very fond of three and who made each aspect of his life a thing of triads. He went home one evening and drank three cups of tea with three lumps of sugar in each, cut his jugular with a razor three times and scrawled with a dying hand on a picture of his wife good-bye, good-bye, good-bye. (AS 217–18)

In one sense symmetry is of the essence here. The three good-byes with which the book ends (and 'good-bye' is as apt a word as any with which to close your first novel) can be said to correspond to its three conclusions, which in number (but not in content) match the three proposed starts of the student's manuscript. Moreover, the numerical theme has received substantial discussion midway through the book, in the Pooka and the Good Fairy's discussions of the moral significance of odd and even numbers (AS 106–10). At the same time, though, this 'Ultimate' conclusion is profoundly disorienting. It's not just that it ends the book on a woeful note of suicide and madness: it's also that the whole shambling sermon floats free of the rest of At Swim, referrable to no familiar source. With the intricate narrative levels shelved, we are floating in space. It's not A, B or C: it might be Z.

Flann O'Brien's debut novel, then, is at once meticulously framed and carelessly unhinged. Even as it ties up loose ends and seeks to register motif and pattern, *At Swim* is also leaving the reader in the middle of nowhere, refusing to make sense. The book combines an impulse toward intricate coherence, and a tendency wilfully to come apart: if its layers seem to open ingeniously onto one another, its pages also frequently open themselves to any old thing. A tension between unity and disunity, craft and randomness, runs through the work. Many of the connections between parts are tenuous at best: frequently, elements of the book are loosely fastened together at one end, but float free at the other.

Finn MacCool is a good example of this. He exists on level B, within the student's writing. But does he really belong to the same book as Trellis? Early in *At Swim*, the student retires to bed and thinks about Finn: and several pages are spent in an *'Extract from my typescript . . . being humorous or quasi-humorous incursion into ancient mythology'* (*AS* 13). This material, parodic of the style and conventions of Irish legend, has a relative autonomy within *At Swim*. Its connection to the world of Trellis and Shanahan is only produced later, by Trellis's employment of Finn (*AS* 61) – an act which seems all the more absurd due to the gap between the two characters' textual worlds. The gap may seem to be closed when Finn, at the fireside with the 'plain men', tells the story of Sweeny (*AS* 64–72), with regular interruptions in a modern Dublin idiom. In a typical instance, Finn's recital of Sweeny's staves –

> Good its water greenish-green
> good its clean strong wind,
> good its cress-green cresses,
> best its branching brooklime

– is immediately followed by Lamont's observation: 'Quick march again . . . It'll be a good man that'll put a stop to that man's tongue', and Furriskey's more tolerant judgement that 'It has to come out somewhere' (*AS* 78). They can hear him, but can he hear them? At times Finn seems to respond to the plain men, as in his description of the traditional punishment for interrupting him (*AS* 72). Yet he relates his tale not at their request but in answer to a request from 'hidden Conán', for 'Finn in his mind was nestling with his people' (*AS* 63). Indeed, according to the student's manuscript, Finn looks 'like a man whose thought was in a distant part of the old world or maybe in another world altogether' (*AS* 62). The other world he occupies, in fact, is that of the tribal storytelling, undisturbed by modernity, early in the book (*AS* 13–20). Finn has walked from those pages to these, from ancient Ireland to Trellis's dwelling at the Red Swan Hotel: yet it appears that he has never really left his own genre. The same is true of Sweeny himself, who begins as a character within Finn's narration, then materializes in the world of the Pooka and the Good Fairy – tumbling, in effect, from C to B. Although the other characters take care of him (*AS* 126–30), Sweeny himself seems unable to engage with their world. In these cases, characters who belong to different generic modes occupy the same page, but are comically unable to recognize or communicate with each other across stylistic barriers. The leakage between textual worlds serves only to highlight their incommensurability.

Giants, fairies and mad poets alongside working-class Dubliners – *At Swim* does not get more fantastical. Yet even in this most anti-realistic aspect of the book, it is possible to find an engagement with the real. The Ireland in which O'Nolan became a writer was the product of nationalist struggle; the literary culture he inherited was that of the Revival. The ideological work of the Revival, as dominated and defined by Yeats, had been a matter of reclamation and heroicization. Venerable traditions and tales had been revived and redisseminated; and the implication was that the true Ireland was the one described by myth. Contemporary Ireland – the land blighted by Catholic shopkeepers as well as England's imperial rationalism – could be judged by comparison to its ancient past, as disclosed in heroic narrative and legend. Yet there might also be a productive interplay between the mythic and the modern: so Yeats wondered, looking back at 1916, in a poem written the year before *At Swim-Two-Birds* appeared.

> When Pearse summoned Cuchulain to his side,
> What stalked through the Post Office?[7]

In a different manner, the Ireland of *At Swim* is likewise occupied by characters mythic and modern, side by side: sometimes communicating, sometimes oblivious to one another. The novel's criss-crossing levels allow Furriskey and Finn MacCool to be juxtaposed, and a comedy to emerge from the contrast. Critics have puzzled over the implications. Does the modernity of the 'plain men' look degraded in comparison to an epic past, or – as Anthony Cronin suggests – are Finn MacCool and Sweeny made properly 'human' by their journey to the realm of the real?[8] Bernard Benstock, in a piece sceptical of O'Nolan's achievement, finds 'both mimetic appreciation and ironic deprecation . . . an envy of the heroic nature of the epic material of the past and a contemporary scorn for the outmoded'.[9] But the use of myth here works to delegitimate myth as a national ideal. The ancient and legendary characters must coexist with the contemporary. In Yeats's poem this means a *re-enchantment* of the contemporary, in which myth lends its purity and puissance to a modern nationalist: in *At Swim*, the comedy of coexistence amounts to a kind of de-enchantment of myth. Both ancient and modern Ireland provide material for discursive fun, parodies which are the more effective for so closely shadowing their sources. In both cases the achievement is in the detail, from Finn's backside against which 'three fifties of fosterlings could engage with handball' (*AS* 9) to the magnificent silliness of Lamont's drawing-room wisdom: 'A wise old owl once lived in a wood, the more he heard the less he said, the less he said the more he heard, let's emulate that wise old bird' (*AS* 79). It would be a mistake to assume that Finn MacCool, in this novel, is any more authentically Irish than John Furriskey: the force of the book is to locate them on the same textual plane. *At Swim*'s self-interrupting rhythms prevent ancient Irish figures from holding cultural authority, or even historical priority: in an important sense, every generic moment is simultaneous, in what O'Nolan told Niall Sheridan was a 'supra-Bergsonian continuum'.[10] To this extent, the novel's play with styles is also a politics of style. In its demystificatory deployment of the mythic, *At Swim* can qualify as an unlikely and perverse kind of realism.

The presence of Finn MacCool and Sweeny may leave structural loopholes and ambiguities, but there are more radical dissonances within the primary narrative. At the start of the novel, the student reads a letter. With the customary italicized heading – '*Mail from V. Wright, Wyvern Cottage, Newmarket, Suffolk*' – it is accordingly reproduced in full. It turns out to be a circular offering racing tips, and packed with commercial hyperbole: 'there will be a GOLDEN OPPORTUNITY to all who act "pronto" and give their bookmaker the shock of his life' (*AS* 12–13). The complete reproduction of the letter might lead us to think it significant: perhaps the race in question will be central to the plot later on? No chance. Or rather, it's *all* chance. The letter really existed: Niall Sheridan gave it to Brian O'Nolan, who promptly incorporated it into his book. As Anthony Cronin records, other documents that came O'Nolan's way enjoyed the same fate (*NLM* 85). The student's first drink prompts a lengthy '*Extract from Literary Reader, the Higher Class, by the Irish Christian Brothers*', on the dangers of alcohol (*AS* 21); later a character reads aloud from *The Athenian Oracle*, 'an old book purchased for a nominal sum on the quays', and a page of *At Swim* is duly filled with a new style, archaic 's' and all (*AS* 102–3). This compositional process is depicted within the novel itself, when the student's friend Brinsley wonders about the appearance of Trellis:

> I did not answer but reached a hand to the mantelpiece and took down the twenty-first volume of my *Conspectus of the Arts and Natural Sciences*. Opening it, I read a passage which I subsequently embodied in my manuscript as being suitable for my purpose. The passage had in fact reference to Doctor Beatty (now with God) but boldly I took it for my own.   (*AS* 30)

Why not? 'The modern novel', we recall, 'should be largely a work of reference': and if the student's manuscript is one instance of this principle, *At Swim* itself is another.

In this context, Niall Sheridan's own reminiscence of the novel's genesis is profoundly revealing. O'Nolan, he recalls, proclaimed in the mid-1930s that 'the principles of the Industrial Revolution must be applied to literature. The time had come when books should be made, not written – and a "made" book had a better chance of becoming a best-seller'. Sheridan, O'Nolan, Denis Devlin and Donagh MacDonagh thus planned work on 'the Great Irish Novel', to be entitled *Children of Destiny*. The four, O'Nolan proposed, would write the book in different sections, 'then stick the pieces together in committee'. As much as possible of the book would be borrowed and rehashed from elsewhere. As such, '*Children of Destiny* would be the precursor of a new literary movement, the first masterpiece of the Ready-Made or Reach-Me-Down School'.[11]

We can detect here the same tendencies we saw at work in the last chapter, in *Blather* and the *Irish Times*. A text written by several hands, dissolving individual authorship into the collective; a blizzard of masks and pretence; a readiness to reuse or parody material from elsewhere; an openness to chance. In imagining a 'Ready-Made School', Sheridan again invites connection with those European avant-garde movements, Dada and Surrealism, which deliberately made art from the detritus of existing texts and images. To make art from randomness was to make 'art' strange: to put its status and value into question, if not crisis. The Irish Ready-Made School, as remembered by Sheridan, is on the verge of performing a similar operation on literature. Indeed, as if the sense of aesthetic hit-and-hope were not emphatic enough, Sheridan's account begins with O'Nolan speculating about chaining a thousand monkeys to a thousand typewriters.

At Swim-Two-Birds was not quite the Great Irish Novel: at least, not the one that the committee had planned. But it does preserve, in modified form, the approach that O'Nolan had conceived for that collective work. The multiplicity of authors, as we have seen, is projected *into* the work: but in his casual inclusion of texts by other people, O'Nolan also maintains the principle of a book composed by many hands. Like the exchanges of letters to the *Irish Times*, *At Swim* was designedly left open to contingency. Like that collective work, it also fed on itself, for Sheridan recalls that as he and O'Nolan discussed the progress of the novel, O'Nolan wrote their discussions into the manuscript: 'I found myself (under the name Brinsley) living a sort of double life at the autobiographical core of a work which was in the process of creation'.[12] The doubling here is even more complex than the structures we have already examined: a discussion of the book goes into the book, and thus becomes part of the object under discussion. A peculiar circularity is involved here, a feedback loop which makes *At Swim* radically open-ended and self-consuming.

The book was thus an extraordinary achievement: not so much for any traditional virtues of unity and harmony, or for the author's single-minded dedication, as for its readiness to be disunified and dissonant, made of many pieces jammed unpredictably together. *At Swim-Two-Birds* takes great aesthetic risks, of which the greatest is the risk of not really being 'aesthetic' at all. Myles na gCopaleen, as we shall see in the concluding chapter, would frequently pour scorn on the idea and institutions of Art; but his creator would never again write a book which so artfully undid the art of fiction.

3

What Goes Around: *The Third Policeman*

The Third Policeman is packed with mysteries, some of them under investigation by its constabulary. But the book itself is the greatest mystery of Brian O'Nolan's career. It seems to have sprung from nowhere; as long as he lived, it went nowhere. But it takes its reader to unimaginable places.

At Swim-Two-Birds had been published in March 1939. Within two months, O'Nolan was meditating on a follow-up. He asked Longman's how soon it was necessary to bring out a second novel, wondering 'whether whatever is forthcoming should come quickly from the point of view of continuity in whatever fragment I have of the public mind or whether a longish interval is unobjectionable' (*NLM* 97). Not for the last time, he can be seen here anxiously attending to his commercial prospects, and relying on the judgement of his publisher, in a way that would seem most out of character in Joyce or Beckett. O'Nolan would never be entirely comfortable in the role of the Artist. Yet he clearly did want to be a novelist: to produce fiction as regularly as was needed to maintain a reputation in the mind of the book-buying public. In the same letter to Longman's he describes the seed of his second novel:

> Briefly, the story I have in mind opens as a very orthodox murder mystery in a rural district. The perplexed parties have recourse to the local barrack which, however, contains some very extraordinary policemen who do not confine their investigations or activities to this world or to any known planes or dimensions. The most casual remarks create a thousand other mysteries but there will be no question of the difficulty or 'fireworks' of the last book. The

whole point of my plan will be the perfectly logical and matter-of-fact treatment of the most brain-staggering imponderables of the policemen. *(NLM 97)*

Much of the finished book is already evident here. The novel never would be very 'orthodox', even in its first pages; but the letter makes clear that from this earliest conception, the book was to combine accessibility and 'imponderability'. There will be no fireworks, no cut-ups: 'difficulty' will be displaced from the bewildering narrative structure of *At Swim* to the intellectual dialogues of *The Third Policeman*. Over-schematically, we can say that complexity of form is replaced by complexity of content. But that division is never reliable, and the oddness of *The Third Policeman* is indeed manifested in narrative and style, as well as in the ideas to which it gives voice.

O'Nolan's publishers considered the book anything but a return to normality. 'We realize', they stated, 'the author's ability but think that he should become less fantastic and in this new novel he is more so' *(NLM 101)*. Their rejection of the novel was the largest setback of his creative life thus far. He attempted to find a publisher in America, but had no more luck. Already, by September 1940, he was doubting the value of the work. He told the American writer William Saroyan that he had 'made a mess of the thing … it's just a good idea banjaxed for the want of proper work and attention and patience' *(NLM 101)*. Anthony Cronin shows that O'Nolan was always liable to such self-doubt. He needed encouragement to persist with extended projects, and his statements about his own work show him repeatedly disparaging what he has written in the past. This was especially true of *At Swim-Two-Birds*, which he spent two decades writing off as a juvenile jape. Soon enough, he was also ready to write off *The Third Policeman*. He began to claim that the manuscript had been lost. He had mislaid it at a dance, on a tramcar, on a train. In the best story the manuscript was blown, one page at a time, out of the boot of a car during a motoring trip around Donegal *(NLM 102)*. There are, as the novel informs us, many strange winds in the world *(TP 33–4)*.

The book remained officially missing until O'Nolan's death in 1966. A year later, his widow Evelyn had secured its publication, with the same London press which had recently produced his late novels. The straightforwardness of the book's eventual appearance seems a sad irony, given the bitter disappointment that its rejection had caused its author. It is morbidly appropriate, too, that a book about life after death could not appear until after the death of its author. O'Nolan's abandonment of the novel after 1940 remains an enigma. Anthony Cronin proposes that the rejection of the novel was a failure that O'Nolan could not admit, within the narrow and gossipy literary world of mid-century Dublin: to avoid losing face, he must claim that he had lost the manuscript (*NLM* 102). After a while, the book may have seemed more a curse than a boon: a burden from the past rather than a resource for the future. For some readers, though, a suspicion lingers that O'Nolan privately disavowed the book because it disturbed him. '[He] seems to have re-read it', writes Hugh Kenner, 'and been unsettled: the first of thousands of readers it has unsettled'. O'Nolan, Kenner suggests, was troubled by the way the book eluded his own understanding, its hints of mysterious meaning beyond his control: more particularly, Kenner ventures, he was disturbed by its cavalier departures from Catholic orthodoxy.[1] But a reader does not need Brian O'Nolan's religious and cultural background to be unsettled by *The Third Policeman*.

THE BEGINNING OF THE UNFINISHED: NARRATIVE CYCLES

'The only good thing about it', O'Nolan wrote to William Saroyan, 'is the plot':

> When you get to the end of this book you realize my hero or main character (he's a heel and a killer) has been dead throughout the book and that all the queer ghastly things which have been happening to him are happening in a sort of hell which he has earned for the killing. Towards the end of the book (before you know he's dead) he manages to get back to his own house where he used to live with another man who helped in the original murder. Although he has been away three days, this other fellow is 20 years older and dies of fright when he sees the other lad

standing in the door. Then the two of them walk back along the road to the hell place and start going through all the same terrible adventures again, the first fellow being surprised and frightened at everything just as he was the first time and as if he had never been through it before. It is made clear that this sort of thing goes on forever – and there you are. (*NLM* 100)

'There you are': O'Nolan writes as though the substance of the novel is contained in this summary. Let us start by taking him at his word and examining the book's plot.

The novel is narrated by a man in his early thirties. 'I was born a long time ago' (*TP* 7), he informs us on the first page, and the rest of the novel moves forward from this point. Swiftly we are told of the parents, who died when the narrator was a child: of his schooling and subsequent travels: of his return to the family farm, which has been quietly commandeered by the man who was supposed to be merely tending it, John Divney (*TP* 7–13). It sounds like the beginning of a *Bildungsroman*: a tale which will take us from childhood to the present, tracing a rising line of development, registering the education of its protagonist. *At Swim-Two-Birds*, we have seen, also hints at such a structure, only to thwart it. *The Third Policeman* will perform a like subversion, but with very different means. The novel will lead us to its end, only to send us back: in that sense the teleology of the *Bildungsroman* is bent out of shape. And while our narrator will encounter many marvels and be told many strange things on his travels, these will not provide any lessons for general edification. On the contrary, the supposed wisdom he hears – somewhat like the ideas with which Alice must contend in Wonderland – is skewed, incredible, contrary to our world as we understand it. In that sense the protagonist's progress is an inverted development, an education in reverse. It may thus be a blessing in disguise that, having reached the end and been sent back to an earlier stage of the story, he appears to have forgotten everything he has seen along the way.

Halfway through chapter 2, the narrator is disturbed to discover that he has forgotten his name. This changes more for him than it does for us, because we never knew his name to begin with. In fact, to say that he has forgotten his name may be to misrepresent the matter: for what he says is that he now has no name at all (*TP* 32–3). Whatever his name has been, it will never be accessible to us. In this he resembles, once more, the narrator of *At Swim-Two-Birds*. Sue Asbee calls this 'a technical feat that deliberately makes discussion of the central character somewhat awkward', and judges that ' "Not naming" helps to prevent overly simple reader sympathy: it is less easy to identify with someone who remains nameless'.[2] Namelessness, on this view, is a small, subtle contribution to the novel's metafictional effect: a way of holding the reader at a distance. In a boldly Homeric move, Keith Hopper has called the narrator Noman.[3] I shall echo and diverge from him in dubbing the figure Anon, another recognition that getting rid of names is harder than it appears.

The reason for Anon's sudden ignorance of his own name is that he is dead. He and Divney have agreed to kill a wealthy local man, Old Mathers, and divide his money between them. They commit the murder on the road one night: Divney secretly hides Mathers' cashbox, giving him the upper hand over Anon. Three tense years later, Divney finally takes Anon to retrieve the box, which he claims to have left under a loose floorboard in Mathers' house. Groping for the box, Anon triggers the turning point of the novel:

> It was some change which came upon me or upon the room, indescribably subtle, yet momentous, ineffable. It was as if the daylight had changed with unnatural suddenness, as if the temperature of the evening had altered greatly in an instant or as if the air had become twice as rare or twice as dense as it had been in the winking of an eye; perhaps all of these and other things happened together for all my senses were bewildered all at once and could give me no explanation.   (*TP* 24)

Read in isolation, this is striking: it seems unmistakable that a major event in the story is being described. But *The Third Policeman* is a crowded series of such apparent cruxes, moments when reality seems to shudder. The novel has already contained things to give us pause: a father, now dead, who only talks to his sheepdog (*TP* 8), a narrator who casually gains a wooden leg (*TP* 10), two men (Divney and Anon, after the murder) who 'never parted company for more than one minute either night or day' (*TP* 13). We are getting used to oddity, and within the next five chapters will have to get used to far odder things than these. In that sense O'Brien successfully obscures the story's key event, swiftly refocusing the narrative on the night's criminal task: the next two sentences immediately after the passage quoted resume the search and conclude 'The box had gone!' (*TP* 24). Easy to miss the change, which happens in the winking of an eye. But things have changed, changed utterly.

Although many strange things happen between this point and the end of the novel, it is only as we approach the conclusion that the ontological shift we have just witnessed becomes explicit. Anon returns to the farm and finds Divney, sixteen years older, at home with his wife. Only the terror-stricken Divney can see him:

> He said I was not there. He said I was dead. He said that what he had put under the boards in the big house was not the black box but a mine, a bomb. . . . He had watched the bursting of it from where I had left him. The house was blown to bits. . . . I was dead for sixteen years.   (*TP* 203)

It is a grim twist on which to end the novel; and unexpected, as we have naturally assumed Anon to be alive all this time. At the same time, it is oddly conventional. There is something of the tupenny horror story about Divney's revelations: or to put it more generously, the novel has suddenly turned out to be Gothic. In a sense, O'Nolan's description of 'a very orthodox murder mystery' is radically inappropriate to this book; but in the end it nonetheless turns out to be unashamed in its use of a generic narrative, this time the ghost story.

O'Nolan was not the first Irish writer to turn the Gothic mode to his own ends, though most of the others had belonged to a Protestant rather than Catholic tradition.[4] What it helps him toward here is the revelation of the novel's peculiar recursive structure. For now the story prepares to turn on its axis. Anon heads back out into a dismal landscape. Drained of memory and personality, he walks 'mile upon mile of rough cheerless road' until he arrives at a scene familiar to us: the police station which has been central to the main body of the book. Not only the scene is familiar: the lengthy description of the police station is repeated, effectively verbatim, from its first appearance (*TP* 55–6). There is one major difference this time: John Divney arrives, newly crossed to the afterlife, and silently joins Anon in entering the police station.

The Third Policeman turns out to be something of a trick – a book whose effectiveness relies on its having misled the reader. Compared to *At Swim-Two-Birds*, it is structurally a one-trick book, which confounds the reader in a single, concentrated final blow. *At Swim* disturbs narrative convention endlessly, to the point where its main narrative can become almost indiscernible; *The Third Policeman* is superficially a more conventional narrative, but one whose conventional character is radically undercut by its ending.

For all its surprise, this ending appears to offer neatness. The implied shape is a circle: to reach the conclusion of the story is to return to its beginning, and begin the trek anew. As O'Nolan put it in a note which the publishers later appended to the novel, 'Hell goes round and round. In shape it is circular and by nature it is interminable, repetitive and very nearly unbearable' (*TP* 207). Narrative here runs along 'time's cycle' rather than 'time's arrow', and in this respect *The Third Policeman* matches Joyce's *Finnegans Wake*, which was published in its final form while O'Nolan was still composing his novel.[5] *At Swim* refuses linearity by disintegrating the narrative line: *The Third Policeman* does so by hooking the end of the narrative on to its beginning, and dashing any hope of progress. In fact it does not quite do this. *Finnegans Wake*, critics tend to concur, begins its first sentence in the middle of its last sentence, looping syntactically from end back to beginning. *The Third Policeman*, on the other hand, ends with the catchphrase of Sergeant Pluck: 'Is it about a bicycle?' (*TP* 206). This phrase's first airing was on Anon's first entry to the police station (*TP* 57). That was in chapter 4: so the first three chapters seemingly exist outside the loop. But surely those chapters were narrated from a point after the events described in the novel? In that case, how can they have an existence prior to the endless cycle that seems to be unfolding?

In at least two senses, in fact, the book does not describe a perfect circle. The clearest complication is the addition of Divney. No wonder O'Brien leaves the novel where he does: in the very next line he would have had to begin developing an encounter between Pluck, Anon and Divney which could hardly avoid diverging from the first scene in the police station. The ensuing story would not, presumably, end up back at the house the two characters have just come from: should they return there, we can assume that they will not find Divney alive as Anon did. Divney's arrival suggests that if hell does go round and round, it regularly picks up new passengers. In a continuing *Third Policeman*, we might reasonably expect any number of newly dead characters to show up, doing unwitting atonement. That prospect might be dismaying, but by definition it would not be wholly repetitive.

In a second sense, too, the book neglects to be fully circular – and suggests that the attempt to establish such a coherent structure may be in vain. The story is told in the past tense, implying that the narration is being performed from a time and place securely beyond the story itself. But this is not possible within the novel's own terms. If Anon is indeed condemned to walk to and from the police station for eternity, then at what point does he tell his story? If hell does go round forever, he can only be telling us the story from within it. But part of the point of the hell, as O'Nolan's letter emphasizes, is that it makes Anon forget what he has previously experienced: and this oblivion makes the narration of the novel impossible. In that respect it is like much else in this book. The hidden non-sense of its structure – its incomplete circularity – is perversely in keeping with the unfathomability of much that we encounter within it.

VERY NEARLY INSOLUBLE PANCAKES: FANTASY LOGIC

Life in a Flann O'Brien novel is never straightforward, but death is mind-blowing. The fate of Anon is not to cease existing, but to be thrown into a parallel universe where few things work the way they did, and many things happen despite being impossible. These include a conversation with the dead Mathers (*TP* 25–38); the sudden appearance of Anon's soul, whom he casually names Joe (*TP* 26); a police barracks which defies spatial dimensions (*TP* 55); a spear so thin that the end of it is invisible and capable of passing harmlessly through a man's hand (*TP* 70); thirty-one chests of descending size, the smaller encased in the bigger, which diminish to the point of invisibility (*TP* 72–6); inaudible music (*TP* 77); a mangle which can stretch light and make it scream (*TP* 110–12); a ceiling whose markings coincidentally provide a detailed map of the parish (*TP* 127); a mechanical Eternity which one enters and leaves via a lift (*TP* 132–47); objects which are incomprehensible to the eye (*TP* 139–40); a colour which is sufficiently new to turn anyone who sees it insane (*TP* 159); a policeman with the face of Mathers (*TP* 189); and a black box which will fulfil any of its owner's wishes (*TP* 195). This list omits the book's most celebrated eccentricity, which just about remains a theory rather than a fact: the idea that people who ride bicycles gradually swap atoms with their vehicles (*TP* 85–94).

In its otherworldly existence, the black box contains not money but omnium, 'the essential inherent interior essence which is hidden inside the root of the kernel of everything and . . . is always the same' (*TP* 113). Who possesses enough of it becomes omnipotent, able to change the world at will. *The Third Policeman*, like the box, is a means of making fantasies manifest. If the book is tinged with Gothic, it also boasts the outlandish imagination of a modern fairy tale. *At Swim*, too, is crammed with flights of fancy, but they are, in an important sense, functions of the text: reality shifts because another book is being written. In *The Third Policeman*, by contrast, boundaries are not so much textual as metaphysical: the reign of fantasy is facilitated by the transition to another plane of existence. The afterlife is an excuse for O'Brien to tinker with reality, rather as a dream makes possible the nonsensical situations of *Alice's Adventures in Wonderland*. As O'Nolan put it in a letter, 'When you are writing about the world of the dead – and the damned – where none of the rules and laws (not even the Law of Gravity) holds good, there is any amount of scope for back-chat and funny cracks' (*NLM* 100). Typically, he bathetically downplays his own achievement: 'funny cracks' gives little hint of the scale of the book's imagination.

Some of the oddities of O'Brien's hell are themselves bathetic: elevated ideas which turn out to have a comically mundane existence. Anon's soul is a caustic companion, reminiscent of *At Swim*'s Good Fairy, who doubts the Sergeant's description of Eternity: *'when we are told that we are coming back from there in a lift – well, I begin to think that he is confusing night-clubs with heaven. A lift!'* (*TP* 130). Eternity itself is indeed not what one would expect, but an engine-room of pig-iron plates, cogs and wires (*TP* 132–5). But the novel's more striking tendency is in the other direction: not effecting the banal realization of an ideal, but straining to *derealize* things – to produce a world beyond imagining. Thus the sight of the police barracks is beyond Anon's belief:

> It did not seem to have any depth or breadth and looked as if it would not deceive a child . . . . I had never seen with my eyes ever in my life before anything so unnatural and appalling and my gaze faltered about the thing uncomprehendingly as if at least one of the customary dimensions was missing, leaving no meaning in the remainder. . . .
>
> As I approached, the house seemed to change its appearance. At first, it did nothing to reconcile itself with the shape of an ordinary house but it became uncertain in outline like a thing glimpsed under ruffled water. Then it became clear again and I saw that it began to have some back to it, some small space for rooms behind the frontage. I gathered this from the fact that I seemed to see the front and the back of the 'building' simultaneously from my position approaching what should have been the side. (*TP* 55)

Vision, it is commonly asserted, is privileged among the senses: we refuse to believe something implausible until we've seen it with our own eyes.[6] The disturbance here is that vision brings news of the unbelievable. The barracks, Anon adds, are like a poorly painted billboard: the viewer should be able to dismiss them as an unrealistic image. But in the landscape of this novel, this unlikely sight has to be credited as real. The onlooker's gaze falters at the contradiction this involves: at being required to believe what can't be believed.

The visual contradictions might be resolved by being made into a temporal sequence: the differing and incompatible views that Anon gets of it are simply views from different places, and thus ultimately not contradictory. But the house's protean character also adds to its challenge, if we take it that it is actually changing before Anon's eyes. There is a suggestion here not merely of different perspectives, but of a malleable reality: a world which takes on incongruous and unexpected new forms as we move through it. Anon's conclusion registers even greater peculiarity: 'the whole morning and the whole world seemed to have no purpose at all save to frame it and give it some magnitude and position so that I could find it with my simple senses and pretend to myself that I understood it' (*TP* 56). Priorities are disquietingly inverted: rather than a building existing in an environment which has preceded it, the world is an artefact that frames the building.

An irony attends this whole disturbing scene. Anon describes a sight which is hard to visualize, hence an oxymoron. But while the barracks is difficult to picture, it is not necessarily so difficult to *write*. Flann O'Brien is free to produce sentences which are grammatical and semantically consistent, but whose contents are conceptually inconsistent. A starker instance of this occurs in 'Eternity', when Policeman MacCruiskeen produces from nowhere a group of objects with a peculiar quality:

> I can make no attempt to describe this quality. It took me hours of thought long afterwards to realize why these articles were astonishing. *They lacked an essential property of all known objects*. . . . these objects, not one of which resembled the other, were of no known dimensions. . . . Simply their appearance, if even that word is not inadmissible, was not understood by the eye and was in any event indescribable. That is enough to say.   (*TP* 139–40)

We are at the limits of language here – and beyond the limits of the visual. Imagine an attempt to make a film of this scene: how could these objects be represented?[7] O'Brien runs through a series of colours which they are not (neither black, nor white, nor anything in between), and exhausts the series of shapes (they are neither shaped nor shapeless), in order to make it impossible for the reader to visualize this point in the novel. The mind's eye, on a rigorous reading, must remain blank for the duration of this passage. O'Brien thus casually inverts a major convention of reading and writing: that a good description should allow the reader to picture what is being described. The objects here are literally unimaginable. Words, it seems, have a margin of licence that visual representations lack: and O'Brien wilfully abuses that licence here, writing words which can only be words, sentences which can never be translated into anything else. The reader is left to make do in language's margin of freedom, which is as blank as the margin of the book.

The novel achieves equally disturbing effect by a contrasting move: the description of the invisible. The police station and the objects of eternity are described in an excess of specification which paradoxically makes them hard to picture. But another class of object is described in terms of its nearness to nullity. The epitome of this is MacCruiskeen's series of chests, which is still not finished: ' "Nobody has ever seen the last five I made because no glass is strong enough to make them big enough to be regarded truly as the smallest things ever made. . . . The one I am making now is nearly as small as nothing" ' (*TP* 76). How small, the scene prompts us to wonder, must something be before it can be said to be non-existent? This borderline is explicitly played on later, when the smallest chest is lost on the floor, and Mr Gilhaney and Anon are given the impossible task of finding it. Gilhaney's gambit is to return what he considers a handful of nothing to MacCruiskeen, who accepts the chest's return, and then tells Anon that Gilhaney has indeed *accidentally* picked up the invisible chest (*TP* 118). The difference between nothing and something, at this level, appears arbitrary, open to anyone to invent. In the previous example, we were at the limits of representation; now we are at the frontier of being and nothingness.

This is enough to make anyone's head hurt, and Anon's frequently does. MacCruiskeen describes a spear so sharp that 'you cannot think of it or try to make it the subject of a little idea because you will hurt your box with the excruciation of it' (*TP* 70). Anon does his best to have such an idea: 'I fastened my fingers around my jaw and started to think with great concentration, calling into play parts of my brain that I rarely used. Nevertheless I made no progress at all' (*TP* 71). *The Third Policeman* is in part a book about thinking – not the stream of consciousness or the hazy reverie, but the attempt to form clear ideas of things which are exceptionally odd. It is fascinated by, and parasitic upon, logic: its wildest fancies – notably Sergeant Pluck's 'Atomic Theory', the basis of the policemen's obsession with bicycles – have their own kind of internal coherence. The book's most comical excursions in this respect are those attributed to Anon's philosophical hero, de Selby.

De Selby is at once pivotal to the plot, and loosely tacked on to the text. Anon commits the murder to acquire money to publish an edition of de Selby's work, and his narrative frequently drifts off into discussions of the savant's ideas. Yet de Selby is the most detached element of the novel: a distant figure known to Anon only through his writing and that of his fiercely competitive commentators. De Selby is effectively outside the world of the novel, and it is thus appropriate that discussion of his life and thought tends to migrate out of the text proper, and into footnotes. The footnote is at once part of the novel and removed from it: a supplement to the primary text, yet also a diversion from it and a rival to it.[8] This second function becomes especially pronounced when footnotes, rather than merely giving citations to imaginary books ('*Golden Hours*, ii, 261', *TP* 22), build up their own momentum and tell stories in their own right – a tendency which climaxes with the enthralling tale of the international battles among de Selby's commentators (*TP* 172–6), which for three pages seizes far more space on the page than the supposedly primary text of the novel. With elaborate tomfoolery, O'Brien allows his main narrative to be occluded: marginal information impudently becomes central, and what ought to be a merely functional tracking of sources momentarily becomes a thrilling novel in its own right.[9] O'Brien is playing once again with issues that fascinated him in *At Swim*: the relations between genres of writing, narrative and information, fiction and fact. 'The modern novel should be largely a work of reference' (*AS* 25): in a sense *The Third Policeman*, with its simulacrum of academic convention and its elaborate invented system of authors and titles, fulfils this injunction more precisely than *At Swim* itself.

De Selby's ideas are a joke to us, but not to anyone in *The Third Policeman*. Like the policemen, he offers a spectacle of weird science and logic gone astray: but if anything, he heightens the comedy of this mode through his stature as scientist and sage, whose experiments are reported at a respectful distance. Night, he holds, is caused not by planetary movements but by the 'black air' that results from volcanic and industrial emissions: sleep is the asphyxiation brought on by these atmospheric conditions (*TP* 120). Some of de Selby's notions are more directly analogous to the world of the policemen. Due to the finite speed of light, he theorizes that mirrors always offer images of the infinitesimally recent past – and hence that a sufficiently extended series of mirrors, reflecting each other, will show an object as it was years ago (*TP* 67). Characteristically, de Selby has put this idea into practice, and found the only limits to be 'the curvature of the earth and the limitations of the telescope' (*TP* 67). Like Sergeant Pluck's Atomic Theory, this proceeds from what sounds like a serious scientific premise; like McCruiskeen's boxes, it suggests an infinitely repeating series, which is also echoed in the repetitive structure of the novel itself.[10]

Part of the comedy of de Selby arises from the constantly growing contradiction, nowhere made explicit, between Anon's high opinion of him and the negative reports which his narrative has to offer of every aspect of his work. Even de Selby's professional commentators can find nothing good to say for his actual ideas. But we should not dismiss de Selby too swiftly. The satire's potency relies not only on the wrongness of his theories, but on their plausibility. He is a man of science, committed not to blind faith but to deductive reasoning and, especially, to empirical verification. His ideas are counter-intuitive, but so is much of the modern science we trust. We know he's wrong, but his fascination lies in our inability easily to say why. It is harder than it looks to pinpoint where the syllogism becomes false, where sense turns to nonsense: a fact that Myles na gCopaleen would frequently exploit in *Cruiskeen Lawn*.

'To use the frigid words of Bassett, "such information, it is to be feared, makes little contribution to serious deselbiana (sic)" ' (*TP* 121–2). It is the small touches that make de Selby's world, from the footnotes' deadpan mimicry of scholarly discourse, down to the titles of de Selby's works. *Golden Hours*, *Country Album* – these ought to be rustic memoirs, not philosophical tracts. And it is this eye for detail which distinguishes *The Third Policeman*: a virtue that O'Nolan badly undersold in claiming that the book's strength was all in its plot. The language of the de Selby sections is uncharacteristic for being written in a self-consciously Standard English. The bulk of the book is far stranger:

> The day was brand new and the ditch was feathery. I lay back unstintingly, stunned with the sun. I felt a million little influences in my nostril, hay-smells, grass-smells, odours from distant flowers, the reassuring unmistakability of the abiding earth. . . . It was a new and bright day, the day of the world. Birds piped without limitation and incomparable stripe-coloured bees passed above me on their missions and hardly ever came back the same way home. (*TP* 44–5)

Adjectives are odd: bees are 'incomparable' (to what?) as well as 'stripe-coloured' (not 'black and yellow', then). So are adverbs: of all the things to do 'unstintingly', lying down seems the least appropriate. What should be a pastoral ease is continually jolted by unfittingly calculating words: the earth's 'unmistakability', birdsong 'without limitation', bees on 'missions'. The writer systematically chooses words which are unconventional enough to be jarring, but not quite wrong enough to break the scene altogether. And there are many more passages like this.

The novel's world is estranged by words: a 'strange country' (*TP* 41) indeed. We may frequently feel that we are reading an unorthodox translation from another language, an impression confirmed by Hugh Kenner: 'The book's verbal mannerisms . . . seem contrived to demonstrate a pressure of Irish usage, notably *learned* Irish usage . . . upon the English that furnishes its dictionary'.[11] O'Nolan, we recall, had written an MA thesis on nature in Irish poetry (*NLM* 65–7). *Cruiskeen Lawn* would provide an affectionate parody of Dublin dialects, but nothing more outlandish than the speech of the policemen – 'It is lucky for your pop that he is situated in Amurikey . . . if it is a thing that he is having trouble with the old teeth' (*TP* 61) – or Anon's encounter with Martin Finnucane (*TP* 45–51). Out of contemporary speech, mock science, folk tradition and wilful mistranslation, *The Third Policeman* invents a new hybrid: a literary English which bears the unmistakable stamp of Ireland.

This deliberately awkward, ceaselessly estranging diction is fitted for a book in which so much is out of joint. *The Third Policeman* regularly asks us to think the unthinkable – an idea which is itself, in fact, not easy to think. The book operates at the edges of possibility, and tampers with them to disconcerting effect. We might invert our puzzlement that Brian O'Nolan stopped seeking a publisher for the novel, and say it's a wonder he tried to publish it at all. For the book's very existence seems to confirm the possibility of the impossibilities it imagines. Better, if the real world is to retain a semblance of reality, that *The Third Policeman* should do as little existing as possible.

4

Literary Fate: *The Poor Mouth*

The Third Policeman is a novel in English that feels like a translation from the Irish. Having failed to publish that, Brian O'Nolan wrote a novel in Irish and refused to translate it into English. There are interesting parallels and echoes between the two texts – the motif of death as 'eternity', the quest for a hoard of treasure – and in their language, too, they seem to form a contrary pair, gazing at each other across the gap of a translation process that had never happened. As O'Nolan's only novel in Irish, *An Béal Bocht* (1941) was a closed book to many of his admirers until 1973, when Patrick C. Power translated it as *The Poor Mouth*. Perhaps the fact of translation would have displeased O'Nolan. Like Samuel Beckett in the same period, he here veers deliberately away from English.[1] But Beckett habitually translated his French back into English. O'Nolan, by contrast, hid a part of himself in the Irish of *An Béal Bocht* for the rest of his life, teasing readers without the language. The book's incomprehensibility to much of its potential audience performed in public one of its central themes: the gap in understanding between Ireland and England, and more especially between Gaelic-speaking communities and outsiders of various kinds. It also made for an ironic inversion of stereotype: the traditionally unlettered Gael is the one in the know, the supposedly sophisticated English at a loss. Yet the book has now been available in English for three decades, and those without Irish (the present writer included) have been able to recognize its importance in O'Nolan's career, as Irish readers always could. Clearly the Irish text has priority, but this chapter will use Power's translation. O'Nolan once remarked that 'the charm of many works is inseparable from their skins',[2] but his book retains much charm, and much force, even in the skin of a second language.

The Poor Mouth is signed 'Myles na gCopaleen', which signals its origins. It was effectively an offshoot of *Cruiskeen Lawn*, the column O'Nolan began under that pen-name in the *Irish Times* in October 1940. The column occupied him until his death, and we shall consider it in detail in the final chapter. The important point here is that the early columns were much preoccupied with the Irish language and the cultural politics surrounding it. For much of 1940 and 1941, the column was in Irish, and it attracted controversy among language revivalists who considered O'Nolan to be denigrating the national tongue. He was, consciously, in an anomalous position. One reason the column had been commissioned was to establish the Irish credentials of a newspaper associated with Protestants and the Anglo-Irish Ascendancy: as a Catholic writing in Gaelic, O'Nolan sent out a new signal about the paper's identity. But some took the satirical playfulness of his contributions not as a celebration of the possibilities of Irish, but as an attack on the language. 'I have heard many adverse comments on Irish', the self-styled 'West-Briton Nationalist' complained in the paper's letter column: 'But you are spewing on it' (*FOB* 185). Critics have differed over whether the correspondent was O'Nolan himself, donning another guise in the search for controversy. But the Irish language was an inherently sensitive issue. In 1893 the foundation of the Gaelic League had formalized the project of reviving the tongue, as a central strategy of 'deanglicization'.[3] Nationalism ever since had stressed the importance of the language in the attempt to rediscover – or reinvent – an Irish identity separate from that of Britain. Patrick Pearse had sought not merely an Irish Republic but one that spoke Gaelic. He had attempted to teach Irish to James Joyce; Douglas Hyde, the founder of the Gaelic League, had been among the tutors of Brian O'Nolan, whose early proficiency in the tongue left him unimpressed at Hyde's attempts to speak it (*NLM* 53–4). After Independence, Gaelic became part of official culture: promoted in education, required for state employment. O'Nolan himself had undergone an Irish oral examination to obtain his Civil Service post (*NLM* 74). The state also encouraged new publication in Irish. 'As texts in the Irish language began to proliferate', writes Jane Farnon, 'Gaelic literature became inextricably bound to state policy. It was the government's aim to promote the Irish language, there was no room for concern for the creative writer, and any type of experimental writing was discouraged'.[4] The status of the language thus became ambiguous. The very association of Gaelic and national identity which was encouraged by successive governments made the language less attractive to those who sought to refuse the official culture of the new state. This number included many writers and intellectuals, not least O'Nolan's own circle. O'Nolan himself, however, had a more ambivalent position. Fluent in Irish since childhood, he seemed to view the use of the language as a personal right rather than an external obligation; and the use of Irish alongside English, as in *Cruiskeen Lawn*, gave an additional dimension to his verbal play. He frequently insisted on the precision possible in Irish (*FOB* 239), but scorned many existing users of the language as inept. *Cruiskeen Lawn* and *An Béal Bocht* thus represented, among other things, attempts to save the language from its most ardent supporters. Patrick C. Power echoes this view, claiming that the novel was supposed to act 'as a cauterisation of the wounds inflicted on Gaelic Ireland by its official friends' (*PM* 6).

Gaelic Ireland, not just Gaelic. As *The Poor Mouth* makes clear, a strong connection was made between the language and the West of the country: the *Gaeltacht* or Irish-speaking regions. Again language stands for a large social idea: the Gaelic-speaking peasants of the West embodied an idealized Ireland of primitive community, traditional values and ethnic purity. The Gael, the West and the language could all be opposed not only to Anglicization but to modernity as such. The consequences of this are central to *The Poor Mouth*'s investigation.

The Poor Mouth looks, from a distance, simpler than O'Nolan's earlier novels, and it is indeed a less varied novel than its two predecessors. Yet the simplicity is misleading: the work is also profoundly self-conscious. Less diverse in tone than *At Swim-Two-Birds*, it is nonetheless a metafictional novel. Like *At Swim*, it is highly intertextual, and explores the importance of narratives with heavy irony. The narrator of *At Swim* disavows

originality in literature: plots and characters, he avers, should
be taken wholesale from other works (*AS* 25). *At Swim* itself is
one exemplification of this theory: *The Poor Mouth* is another.
The novel draws on a range of previous writing, spinning its
place in an intricate web of allusion. Jane Farnon has argued
that the novel's sources go back as far as the ninth century.[5]
More immediately, it reacts to a spate of memoirs of life in the
West. These include the work of Séamus Ó Grianna, Peig
Sayers, and Peadar Ó Laoghaire, who is mentioned in the text.
The most significant source was *The Islandman*, by Tomás Ó
Criomhthain, published in Irish in 1929 and translated into
English in 1934. Myles publicly acknowledged its effect in
Cruiskeen Lawn: 'The book was published about 1930 and
disturbed myself so much that I put it away, a thing not to be
seen or thought about and certainly not to be discussed with
strangers. But its impact was explosive'.[6] This is not just
Mylesian irony: in a letter almost twenty years after his novel
had been published, O'Nolan described *An Béal Bocht* as 'an
enormous jeer at the Gaelic morons here with their bicycle
clips and handball medals, but in language and style ... an
ironical copy of a really fine autobiographical book' (*FOB* 235).
Clearly the complexity of O'Nolan's relation to Irish is enacted
in his response to the source texts. *The Poor Mouth* is anything
but a simple tribute or imitation, but it is not necessarily
contemptuous of its targets either. As Sue Asbee remarks, 'Our
ideas of parody have to be adjusted' in this case,[7] and
O'Nolan's own phrase 'ironical copy' might point towards the
subtlety required.

Scholars have shown that the textual format of *The Poor
Mouth* is riddled with allusions to *The Islandman*. The title page
of Ó Criomhthain's book had included a quotation from the
body of the text: 'Our likes will never be again'. Myles picks
up this refrain in his own work, but also quotes his own book
on the title page: 'If a stone is thrown there is no predicting
where it will land' (*PM* 3). Ó Criomhthain also commences
each chapter with a list previewing the events to follow. This
is a generic device available within the novel tradition, but
Myles' own versions of such lists are almost certainly an
imitation of Ó Criomhthain (*FOB* 246–7). Yet for all Ó
Criomhthain's importance as a precursor to be mined and

tweaked, *The Poor Mouth*'s greatest significance is not as a rewriting of a particular book, but rather a reinscription of a *genre*. If *The Islandman* had been a one-off, *The Poor Mouth* would lose much of its point. The novel is concerned to show, not that the Gaels have produced one colourful memoir, but that their life has been written over and over again in the same way. The Gael has become a groove, a convention, a cliché. The term in *The Poor Mouth* which best catches this is 'literary fate', as the Old-Grey-Fellow uses it in the Rosses:

> – Is it the way, said I finally, that there's no one alive in this countryside or is it that they're all cleared out from us to America? Whatever way things are in this part of the world, all the houses are empty and everyone away from home.
> – 'Tis clear, wee little son, said the Old-Fellow, that you haven't read the good books. 'Tis now the evening and according to literary fate, there's a storm down on the seashore, the fishermen are in difficulties on the water, the people are gathered on the strand, the women are crying and one poor mother is screaming: Who'll save my Mickey? That's the way the Gaels always had it with the coming of night in the Rosses.   (*PM* 66–7)

'Fate' is among the novel's recurrent words. The Gaels of Corkadoragha are resigned to their world of endless rain and perpetual potatoes; its cyclical character is hinted at by the appearance at the end of Bonaparte's 'father', who has just served the same twenty-nine-year stretch in the same prison that the protagonist is about to enter. What Declan Kiberd calls an 'inexorable logic of idiotic predestination' steers the narrative:[8] in the Old-Fellow's representative words, 'There's no use for us trying to escape from fate, oh bosom friend!' (*PM* 81). Yet fate is also 'literary' in conforming to narratives and scenes laid down in advance. The way to understand the land of the Gaels, it seems, is to read 'the good books' already published about them. This seems a plausible, if risky, assumption in the real world, where people in Dublin, let alone London, might gain their knowledge of the West from memoirs and stories. (In the example above, Synge's *Riders to the Sea* seems to be one of the 'good books' in question.) But it becomes a manifest absurdity when used as a maxim in this fictional world, which is the world of the Gaels themselves. The characters of the

65

book are not only pre-scripted, but consciously so: experienced characters like the Old-Fellow are aware that everything in this world follows literary cliché. Bonaparte's error, absurdly, is not to have read enough conventional, predictable narratives about his own environment.

In this sense the book is powerfully self-conscious, to a degree not always stressed by commentary on it. The Gaels of the novel are simple folk, trapped in their endless cycle of showers and spuds: but they are also metafictional figures, who effectively step out of role to give ironic recognition of the generic conventions in which they exist. The book does not simply replay stereotypes, it foregrounds them to striking effect. This practice can go out of its way for comic purposes, as in the early incident when the Old-Fellow orders Bonaparte's mother not to sweep the house:

'When I was a raw youngster growing up, I was (as is clear to any reader of the good Gaelic books) a child among the ashes. You have thrown all the ashes of the house back into the fire or swept them out in the yard and not a bit left for the poor child on the floor. . . . It's an unnatural and unregulated training and rearing he'll have without any experience of the ashes.' (*PM* 16)

The acquiescent mother 'took a bucket full of muck, mud and ashes and hen's droppings from the roadside and spread it around the hearth gladly in front of me':

When everything was arranged, I moved over near the fire and for five hours I became a child in the ashes – a raw youngster rising up according to the old Gaelic tradition. Later at midnight I was taken and put into bed but the foul stench of the fireplace stayed with me for a week; it was a stale, putrid smell and I do not think that the like will ever be there again. (*PM* 16)

The important point here is that verisimilitude has been sacrificed for cliché – by the characters themselves. Having achieved a clean house, the Gaels must forego it, for it violates the romantic memoirist's figure of speech: and the child is thus allowed to wallow in a cliché which has been not so much 'literalized' as grossly materialized.

An even more elaborate version of the joke occurs in the trip to the Rosses, when Bonaparte gathers the following advance information:

Some were always in difficulty; others carousing in Scotland. In each cabin there was: i) one man at least, called the 'Gambler', a rakish individual, who spent much of his life carousing in Scotland . . . ii) a worn, old man who spent the time in the chimney-corner bed and who arose at the time of night-visiting to shove his two hooves into the ashes, clear his throat, redden his pipe and tell stories about the bad times; iii) a comely lassie named Nuala or Babby or Mabel or Rosie for whom men came at the dead of every night with a five-noggin bottle and one of them seeking to espouse her. (*PM* 65)

It is a cartoon world, where people are condemned to play two-dimensional roles. The reader should not be too surprised when each of the stereotypes is encountered, but the sureness of O'Nolan's comic touch is visible – as in the paragraph, ticking through clichés, which winds to the conclusion: 'She had a son named Mickey (his nickname was the *Gambler*) but he was carousing yonder in Scotland' (*PM* 68).

The serious thought beyond the laughter is that people are living by these worn scripts – or, if they're not, that we might be diminishing them by imagining that they are. 'He who thinks I speak untruly', warns Bonaparte, 'let him read the good books, or the *guid buiks*' (*PM* 65). O'Nolan is in some respects a bookish writer, whose texts refer to other texts as much as to the real life we readily counterpose to them. But in *The Poor Mouth* this trait is set to work against itself: through his knowledge of books, he asks about the distortions that they have perpetrated. This story is made from other stories – but in the process it casts suspicion on their effects, their ability to prescribe the world. The critique of literary merit is also a critique of national imagination: why can Ireland imagine no other fates for the Gael?

That language is a tool for constructing worlds is suggested elsewhere in the book. This can emerge in a comedy of mistranslation. The Old-Fellow says Bonaparte's father is in the jug, and our credulous hero looks without avail in the milk jug (*PM* 15). A small jest, but improved when we learn that Irish makes no equivalence between prison and pitcher. The Old-Fellow, speaking Gaelic as he is, could not really have created this ambiguity: it's the pure product of the author's play back and forth between languages.⁹ But there are more sinister cases. Bonaparte goes to school – wearing, according to Myles' deliberate misinterpretation of the Gaelic memoir, *nothing but* grey-wool breeches, and alongside children who have, impossibly, crawled along the road or swum from Aran – and is immediately asked his name (*PM* 29–30). His answer is an extravagant genealogy: 'Bonaparte, son of Michelangelo, son of Peter, son of Owen, son of Thomas's Sarah', and so on. The teacher cracks his skull with an oar, in order to impress upon him his new name: 'Jams O'Donnell' (*PM* 30). In a work satirical of the Gaelic revival, this scene is a brutal reminder of the coercion through which Gaelic was lost in the first place. Every child suffers the same fate: English, then, may imply as grimly monotonous a world as Gaelic.

The book's most trenchant satire is directed at Gaelic revivalists, 'Gaeligores', who arrive from outside to study and record Gaelic terms and customs. They speak fluent English, 'but they never practised this noble tongue in the presence of the Gaels lest, it seemed, the Gaels might pick up an odd word of it as a protection against the difficulties of life' (*PM* 48). That sums up a main line of this novel's polemic. The rest of Ireland wants an authentic Gaelic remnant, and does not want that remnant polluted by progress, even if that simply means a decent standard of living. The book is uncompromising about the poverty faced by the Gaels: Bonaparte decides that it would be better to die seeking his fortune than 'to live at home famished in the centre of the plain' (*PM* 103). In a sense the book risks playing along with the aestheticization of that poverty, albeit by making it comic rather than picturesque. But it is scathing about those who would preserve Gaelic hardship as a safe source of cultural purity. The Gaeligores are even more tied to the script than the Gaels: when the Old-Fellow asks whether they are leaving because the local Gaelic has declined, the Gaeligore responds that the word decline is not to be found in the canonical Gaelic works of Father Peter O'Leary (*PM* 49). Contemporary reality is being overridden by textual convention – as it is, still more brutally, when Bonaparte's intended tries to escape her marriage: 'Mabel was in the end of the house at this juncture with my mother on top of her. The poor girl was trying to escape back to her father's

house and my mother endeavouring to make her see reason
and to submit to her Gaelic fate' (*PM* 84). Amid the grotesque-
rie we almost glimpse a human being, crushed to death by the
stereotypes. That also happens, more ludicrously, at the Gaelic
feis which the Old-Fellow organizes to attract the Gaeligores.
They come from Dublin and Galway city, with Gaelic costume
that looks unfamiliar to the Gaels, and new names. 'The Little
Brown Hen' and 'Roseen of the Hill' are evident attempts to be
more Gaelic, but 'Popeye the Sailor' and 'The Dative Case'
have also slunk into the list, tilting it towards chaos in a nod
back to the catalogues of *Ulysses* (*PM* 52–3). A man who
appears 'suspended between deaths from two mortal diseases'
has dubbed himself 'Gaelic Daisy' and been elected President
of the Feis. He it is who is most devastatingly allowed to
condemn himself:

> 'May I state that I am a Gael. I'm Gaelic from the crown of my head
> to the soles of my feet – Gaelic front and back, above and below.
> Likewise, you are all truly Gaelic. We are all Gaelic Gaels of Gaelic
> lineage. He who is Gaelic, will be Gaelic evermore. . . . There is
> nothing in this life so nice and so Gaelic as truly true Gaelic Gaels
> who speak in true Gaelic Gaelic about the truly Gaelic lan-
> guage.' (*PM* 54–5)

We remember that this was written in Gaelic. The attack, via
tautologies which approach the infinities of *The Third Policeman*, is not on the language, or on those who happen to speak
it, but on the self-reflecting, opportunistic emptiness of the
rhetoric that so abstractly promotes it. Why, wonders Myles na
gCopaleen in the *Irish Times*, need the Irish assert their
Irishness?

> I know of no civilisation to which anything so self-conscious could
> be indigenous. Why go to the trouble of proving that you are Irish?
> Who has questioned this notorious fact? If, after all, you are not
> Irish, who is? (*AW* 145)

Perhaps the answer is, the Gaels – several of whom are
crushed to death due to their inability to keep up with the
Gaelic Long Dance (*PM* 59). But the Gaels, awkwardly, will not
quite stand still in the stereotypes that the Gaeligores have
brought. Far from desiring a simple subsistence unblemished

by greed, they are mercenary. The Old-Fellow organizes the Feis to make money (*PM* 50), and steals the President's 'yellow watch' (*PM* 61); more strikingly, and contrary to their ideological image, the family make several pounds out of an English inspector by asserting shamelessly that their pigs are English-speaking children (*PM* 35–7). The desperate opportunism of the Gaels here interacts with a confusion of animal and human which, as Declan Kiberd notes, had been a long-standing motif in English representations of the Irish.[10]

So the novel snipes both at colonial stereotypes and at the cultural purism of post-colonial Ireland. It accuses modern Ireland of using the Gaels to ease its conscience, while excluding them from modernization. Dublin, the book implies, has needed to point to the Gaeltacht as a locus of purity: but that purity is unreal, for those Gaels who are well-fed enough to stand up are seeking to exploit the benefits of their 'native' status, and thus eroding it in the same gesture. The impoverished Gaels need to be cunning: the rest of Ireland needs them to be both impoverished and uncalculating, and this is an unreasonable demand. The book hardly endorses modernity, either. It is the urban sophisticates who play at being Gaels, in ways which make the Gaels wonder whether they themselves are insufficiently Gaelic (*PM* 51–2). Myles na gCopaleen is here in the business of debunking, not making positive proposals. But the novel does suggest, amid the laughter, that picturesque poverty is not the right price to pay for a nation's self-image. Myles' like will not be there again: but he has inspired successive generations of writers who have used comedy, not to dodge or dissolve difficult issues, but to ask questions about Ireland's idea of itself.

5

The Ends of Narrative: *The Hard Life* and *The Dalkey Archive*

The Poor Mouth is subtitled 'A bad story about the hard life'. When Brian O'Nolan returned to writing fiction almost two decades later, he reused that last phrase as the title of his new novel. The reader may well wonder whether that was an ominous sign that he had run out of imaginative energy. The novel itself does not give an encouraging answer. At least its material was all new, which is more than can be said for the last published novel, *The Dalkey Archive* (1964), a book that draws on material that proved to be from the late 1930s. The critical status of these last two novels is moot. Both were fairly well reviewed on first publication, and both have been praised more recently. Anthony Cronin calls *The Hard Life* 'a small masterpiece' (*NLM* 217); one biography describes *The Dalkey Archive* as 'the author's favourite, a preference shared by many of his readers' (*IB* 130). Both novels have been dramatized: Hugh Leonard had made *The Dalkey Archive* into the successful play *The Saints Go Cycling In* within months of its publication. But the contrast between these late novels and the trilogy with which O'Nolan began is sharp, and unflattering. The final works were published in what would prove to be the last five years of O'Nolan's life, after many years away from the genre. On top of his excessive drinking, the period saw him afflicted with various ailments, including a broken leg, and he was increasingly in and out of hospital. Never mind the novels' qualities: we might say that the wonder is they were written at all. They represented an Indian summer in O'Nolan's writing life, a late burst of good fortune and creativity in a career which had increasingly seemed to be ebbing away. This may well be one reason for their relatively favourable reception, and the harshest critic would not want to strip O'Nolan of this late solace. But as Tess Hurson has well observed in relation to *The Hard Life*, their deficiencies can actually put the earlier achievements in clearer relief.[1] This chapter will deal with the last two novels in turn, and place them in the context of the rest of his work.

POINTLESS ENOUGH: *THE HARD LIFE*

What prompted the return to novel-writing was the unexpected return of *At Swim-Two-Birds*, reissued by MacGibbon and Kee in 1960. The same firm published the last two novels, and in writing these O'Nolan remained in regular dialogue with Timothy O'Keeffe, the admirer who had brought *At Swim* back to public attention. If *At Swim* did spur him back into action, it was not so much as a reminder of his literary powers, more as an irritation to be vanquished. He dismissed his first novel, by now, as a schoolboy prank: *The Hard Life* was to show what he could do as a man of 50. To that extent it should not surprise us that *The Hard Life* is not an experimental anti-novel. 'All the persons in this book are real', reads its epigraph, 'and none is fictitious even in part' (*HL* 7). This is characteristic in its inversion of a norm: and as the norm it inverts is a legal precaution, it also ties in with O'Nolan's hope that the book would earn notoriety by being banned (*NLM* 213–14). The epigraph may also reflect the covert real-world provenance that Peter Costello and Peter van de Kamp claim for certain places and characters in the novel (*IB* 122). Tess Hurson sees it slightly differently, as a signal of the book's deliberate turn from the fictional intricacies of the earlier works and towards a kind of realism. *The Hard Life*, she suggests, 'refuses fictionality'.[2]

Certainly it refuses the kind of fictionality offered by *At Swim*. It is effectively a book of one level: the real world, as reported by the young narrator Finbarr. There are no Pookas, no deliberately mechanical recaps of the plot, no recursive ending to send us back to the start. Like the earlier novels this is a first-person narrative: but this narrative goes unmolested by other voices or metafictional games. Finbarr mediates everything – and this is central to the novel's weakness. On one hand, Finbarr is a weak character: undistinguished, lacking in personality or drive, to the point of transparency. He ends the book with no particular plans, but having inherited money: 'I suppose that five hundred pounds will give me at least another two years to think about it if I need all that time' (*HL* 124). He seems unlikely to have any brainwaves however many years he takes. On the other hand, the novel does nothing to place or ironize this nonentity: it offers us no way of seeing round him. O'Nolan, in a letter, called him 'a complete ass'.[3] But the novel itself gives no clue that the reader should see through and disdain Finbarr: he is not a self-evidently unreliable narrator. And it offers no alternative vantage point for the reader: the story does not consistently work to undermine his perceptions. However much of an ass he may be, the reader must take him or leave the book. In its unsteady misuse of a first-person narrator, *The Hard Life* manages to botch something that the earlier novels had turned to their advantage. And this is a general feature of the late fiction: what distinguished the earlier works is here inverted, misapplied or exposed. We shall see this happening in different ways during this chapter.

The earlier novels in their different ways all parodied the *Bildungsroman*: *The Hard Life* almost performs it straight. Only almost: because this is still a comic novel rather than a slice of naturalism. Hurson's claim that the characters are 'too life-like to submit to fictionalisation'[4] omits the element of caricature at work – but it is true that this sense of caricature derives less from vivid characterization than from the roles that the different figures occupy in the plot.

In 1890 the brothers Finbarr and Manus are orphaned: the book's first page, like the opening of *The Third Policeman*, recounts a dim memory of their vanished parents (*HL* 11). As critics have pointed out, the absence of family is a feature of all O'Nolan's fiction: fathers, in particular, have disappeared before the start of every book.[5] Yet *The Hard Life* does immediately supply a kind of surrogate family, as Manus and Finbarr are transported to the home of their half-uncle Mr Collopy, his wife Mrs Crotty, and his daughter Annie. The rest of the novel tells of the intertwined fates of these characters. Finbarr and Manus are both sent to school with the Christian Brothers, until Manus leaves to become an ingenious, crooked entrepreneur. Mrs Crotty sickens and dies, intensifying Mr Collopy's obsession with his personal crusade. This cause is never named directly during the book, but it becomes evident that Mr Collopy's aim is to provide public toilets for women: he considers the lack of the amenity an affront to civilization. His foil in discussing this and other matters – notably the history of the church – is the German Jesuit priest Kurt Fahrt.

When Collopy falls ill, Manus sends him a patent medicine, 'Gravid Water', intended to restore his weight. Finbarr mistakenly administers too much medicine, swelling Collopy's weight to an absurd 29 stone (*HL* 96). Manus writes from London that only a divine cure is possible, and arranges to take Collopy and Fahrt on a pilgrimage to Rome. We hear about the results through Manus's letters. Collopy uses the papal audience to bring up his lavatorial campaign, outraging the Pope; due to his weight he subsequently crashes through a stairwell and dies. Manus has him buried in Rome and returns to Dublin to hear Collopy's will. He leaves Finbarr with the apparently unwelcome suggestion that he marry Annie.

What is evident from this synopsis is that the book combines the sordid and the fantastic. *The Hard Life* misses no opportunity to wallow in historical grime. It may be no accident that it depicts a similar period and setting to Joyce's *Dubliners*. Joyce had written of the 'odour of corruption' that he hoped hung over his stories:[6] O'Nolan subtitled *The Hard Life* 'An Exegesis of Squalor'. The novel is fixated on the body in its most repellent and abject aspects: urine, skin complaints, sexually transmitted disease. To this extent it qualifies better than *At Swim* as a 'schoolboy' production – as the glee with which O'Nolan named Father Fahrt demonstrates (*NLM* 214). The book's last words, provoked by Manus's bright idea, are 'a tidal surge of vomit' (*HL* 126).

Yet the novel is also peculiarly fanciful. Manus's runaway success, which originates in his invisible tightrope walking; Gravid Water; the audience with the Pope – these ideas belie any bid for realism, and nudge the novel into the exaggerating genres of satire and farce. *The Hard Life* is farcical in its silliness, in the chortling naughtiness of its inventions; it is satirical insofar as its comedy mocks institutions and customs, not least ecclesiastical ones. Combined with the naturalistic urban background, these tendencies make for a hybrid work: an exegesis of squalor, perhaps, but also an exercise in toilet humour.

It is an uneven work, which splices genres together and veers between different tones. That describes some of the triumph of *At Swim-Two-Birds*, but also the failure of *The Hard Life*. The central paradox of late Flann O'Brien is that what distinguished his debut anti-novel spoils his attempts to write plain novels. Pedantry was richly comic in the absurd lists and endless mistranslations of *At Swim*: now it surfaces in Collopy's hectoring, point-scoring exchanges with Fahrt (*HL* 60–68). The jagged transitions of *At Swim* ('Conclusion of the Foregoing') here become wayward waverings in tone. And the first novel's model of writing as cut-up and collage also has its echo in *The Hard Life*. Central to Manus's money-making is the copying and replication of other people's texts, which he sells to a credulous mail-order public as the work of the 'London University Academy' (*HL* 72). The first instance of this method is his guide to tightrope-walking, which Finbarr reads and reproduces for us: 'It were folly to asseverate that periastral peripatesis on the *aes ductile*, or wire, is destitute of profound peril not only to sundry *membra*, or limbs, but to the back and veriest life itself' (*HL* 40) – and so it goes on. Here is O'Nolan's old delight in stylistic performance, and in the pseudonym: the extract is attributed to 'Professor Latimer Dodds', which Finbarr considers a mere cover for Manus (*HL* 41). As the operation expands, Manus republishes material like the 'Odes and Epodes of Horace done into English Prose by Dr Calvin Knottersley, D.Litt (Oxon)', drawn from 'his private mine, the National Library' (*HL* 57). When he reaches London he sends Finbarr a long list of subjects in which he now offers correspondence courses: Boxing, Oil Prospecting, Railway Engineering, and much more, including the giveaway 'A Cure For Cancer' (*HL* 82). 'We really aim', Manus writes, 'at the mass-production of knowledge' (*HL* 83).

This is the clearest continuity between early Flann O'Brien and late. The Irish Ready-Made School, we recall, had aimed to make books with the efficiency of the industrial age: 'Existing works would be plundered wholesale for material'.[7] Manus applies a similar logic to education, and the motive is similarly mercenary. Here, then, O'Nolan's ideas from the mid-1930s are still discernible: but they are put into a novel which, unlike *At Swim*, aims to maintain a single textual level. The extensive inclusion of Manus's letters (*HL* 82–6, 91–4, 96–7, 98–9, 103–5, 106–7, 107–12, 115–17) itself echoes the earlier novel's framing of text within text: they effectively commandeer the last third of *The Hard Life*. But O'Nolan handles them uncertainly. Manus is granted control of the narrative, but his discourse meanders more than Finbarr's has done, and the text is dotted with redundant epistolary mechanics: 'I'll write soon again. Pass on to me any news that arises' (*HL* 86), 'Please attend to all these matters without fail and send me a telegram if there is any hold-up' (*HL* 99), and the like. The narrative loses directness, but does not gain fresh voice or complexity in exchange. Among the most pitiful moments of Brian O'Nolan's entire career are the lame, half-hearted comments that Finbarr adds at the close of two of the letters: 'I sighed and put the letter in my pocket. There was not much in it really' (*HL* 86), and worse still, 'Well, that was a long and rather turgid letter' (*HL* 94). So what, we may ask, is it doing in the novel? *The Hard Life* is undecided what to make of its own turgidity. As if losing his nerve, O'Nolan has his narrator dismiss what he has just written. Neither plausible nor metafictional, neither compelling nor able to make a joke of dullness: we are in the worst of all worlds.

Yet *The Hard Life* does develop the Flann O'Brien canon in its representation of two subjects largely absent from the early fiction: women and the church. Indeed these topics are not altogether separable. Keith Hopper argues persuasively that O'Nolan's entire canon is marked by an anxious reticence about sexuality, and women, which betrays its roots in a society dominated by a draconian Catholic church.[8] Few women have noteworthy roles in his fiction: those who do are handled awkwardly at best, and sometimes worse – as in the disturbingly casual references to sexual assault in *At Swim-Two-Birds* (*AS* 61). In this context, *The Hard Life* is a step forward, but a very uncertain one. Finbarr's naïve narration gives O'Nolan an alibi for reticence. He presents sexuality as a mystery, as when the suspicion arises that Annie has become a prostitute: 'What was the meaning of this thing sex, what was the nature of sexual attraction? Was it all bad and dangerous?' (*HL* 90). This passage may partly be a parody of Joyce's depiction of sexual awakenings in *Dubliners* and *A Portrait*. But it fails to offer any answers to its own questions. Finbarr almost writes to Manus about his feelings for Penelope – 'But reason, thank God, prevailed. I said nothing but signed and sealed the letter' (*HL* 91). Here the novel is almost explicit about its own internal censorship.

The omission may be just as well, for what we do see of Penelope is another weak spot in the O'Nolan *oeuvre*: 'Did card games attract me much? I don't know but Jack's sister, Penelope . . . certainly did. She was what was known as a good hoult, with auburn hair, blue eyes and a very nice smile. And to be honest, I think she was fond of myself' (*HL* 73). The perennial uniqueness of romance is smothered by the retreat to convention: that phrase 'what was known as' executes the flight from emotion and into dismissive, embarrassed chit-chat. The one conversation with Penelope herself receives the kiss of death we have already observed, the narratorial dismissal – 'Our conversation, as may be seen, was trivial and pointless enough, and the rest of it was that kind' (*HL* 89) – and she soon disappears from the novel altogether. Her only significance has been to offer the unattainable, virginal object of a desire which the novel is unable to contain – which its author doesn't really know how to handle.

In one sense women are unusually central to *The Hard Life*: Mr Collopy's campaign on their behalf is basic to the plot. It is hard to be sure what value we are supposed to attach to this crusade. Certainly Collopy's vehemence about the cause is supposed to be the object of laughter: to that extent, as critics have argued, the book works against his liberal progressivism.[9] But the novel also gives his polemics more space than it can take back. When he tells Father Fahrt that the church is fond of suffering as long as someone else is doing it (*HL* 29), his argument has a ring of conviction that mockery cannot dispel. O'Nolan himself may have been unsure about his attitude to Collopy and his cause; but Collopy has a rhetorical appeal, as the centre, in this novel, of the Dublin idiom that fascinated the author. As Anthony Cronin observes, 'He, more than the brother or the narrator, is the book's informing spirit, the comic creation which makes us remember it with affection': to that extent Cronin's sense that 'the author seems to be on Mr Collopy's side' (*NLM* 217) is plausible.

The other side, here, is the church, which in the form of Father Fahrt forms Collopy's most visible antagonist. The plot pits Collopy's humane reformism against a transcendentalism which would ignore human suffering: the latter certainly emerges no better than the former. Father Fahrt, the mendicant Jesuit, is as addicted as Collopy to the 'crock' of whiskey that they share: the church is more worldly and compromised than it would like to admit. But as Keith Hopper notes, if the novel is intended as 'a critique of the Irish Catholic experience', then 'it fails through coyness, reticence and disorganisation of resources'.[10] The plainest instance of coyness is the audience with the Pope himself. To write this at all was as daring as O'Nolan could get: it is telling that the incident is narrated in a letter from Manus. It is thus placed at a remove: O'Nolan fractionally disengages himself from the responsibility of authoring it. The whole set-piece is further distanced from us through the peculiar rendition of the dialogue, in which the Pope's comments are rendered in Italian before an English translation. He is loftily dismissive of Collopy's entreaties, speaking a discourse of institutional authority rather than a humanized, humorous idiom. (We can contrast this with *The Dalkey Archive*'s representation of St Augustine, whose speech comically has a Dublin inflection.) It is hard to say that the Pope loses any authority from his appearance here. And that is finally also true of Catholicism itself. If the novel dares to pick at the church's history, its centrality is also felt more strongly here than in any previous O'Brien novel. In Cronin's words, 'The jokes are to a large extent irreverent, but they presuppose something to be reverent about' (*NLM* 216–17).

Manus's parting suggestion that Finbarr marry Annie is intended to tie everything up: instead it brings everything up. In its ambiguity, Finbarr's emetic response is perhaps the novel's strongest image. He vomits at what feels like the radical incongruity of the idea: Keith Hopper rightly calls it an expression of sexual disgust, characteristic of the author's wariness of women.[11] But the 'tidal surge' of 'everything inside me', and the climactic placing of the act at the novel's end, suggest something more: as though Finbarr's recoil here performs a final revulsion at the whole book, and all the squalor and failure it contains. In that sense, it is *The Hard Life*'s most lucid moment.

THE LAST LAUGH: *THE DALKEY ARCHIVE*

Even the weaknesses of *The Hard Life* could hardly prepare us for the oddness of its successor. Like Flann O'Brien's other works, it mixes the familiar and the strange to unusual effect. The novel takes place in and around Dublin, particularly in the southern suburb named in its title. The central character, Mick Shaughnessy, is a civil servant as his author had been; he spends time drinking with his cynical friend Hackett and dithering about his relationship with his comparatively soph-isticated girlfriend Mary. Normality is disturbed when Mick and Hackett encounter De Selby, a Dalkey-based savant who has developed a substance ('DMP') which removes oxygen from the atmosphere. De Selby has used this invention to call up figures from the past: in an undersea cave he demonstrates it to Mick and Hackett by summoning Saint Augustine to be interrogated on theological history. The more significant func-tion of DMP, however, will be to destroy all life on Earth, in retribution for the destructiveness of humanity (*DA* 18).

Mick's attempt to prevent the end of the world is thus the novel's centre, around which sub-plots and extra characters are drawn in. Father Cobble, an English Jesuit priest, meets De Selby to little effect; the local policeman Sergeant Fottrell, more usefully, helps Mick to break into De Selby's house and steal the canister of DMP, which is then secured in the Bank of Ireland. Most significant is the appearance of James Joyce, who Mick learns is still alive and living in the nearby seaside resort Skerries. Joyce turns out to be a pious man who disavows writing *Ulysses* and *Finnegans Wake*, and wants to join the Jesuits and continue his work on theology. Mick plans to introduce him to De Selby, hoping that they will collaborate on an incomprehensibly obscure book which will keep them occupied and prevent the destruction of all life. This conceit comes to nothing, however, as De Selby's abrupt departure for England is announced. His house is suddenly destroyed by a fire, and the three young characters promptly revert to domestic quarrels and arrangements.

Synopsis can make a novel sound more awkward and disconnected than it is in the experience of reading. With *The Dalkey Archive* the risk is reversed: to summarize its plot may make it sound more coherent than it really is. To list the book's characters and events is to play with absurdity. O'Nolan had always done that: the surprise here is how loosely the absurdities are bound together, how flimsily and inadequately the narrative joins its disparate whimsies. Like *The Hard Life*, it is a realist novel in that it operates on one level: Joyce, De Selby, Fottrell and the ordinary Dubliners must coexist without the excuse of frame-breaking devices or multiple worlds. Yet the coexistence is uneasy: although the plot connecting them is relatively elaborate, the varied scenes and characters often seem to belong to their own private narratives, which have been tugged into the frame of a single novel. This is most literally true of the materials which O'Nolan pulls from the unpublished typescript of *The Third Policeman*.[12] De Selby at last appears in person, though this version is more threatening than the comical rationalist referred to in the earlier work. Sergeant Fottrell is a reincarnation of Sergeant Pluck (whose name has migrated to another policeman (*DA* 50–51)), with a different body ('tall, lean, melancholy', *DA* 46) but similarly eccentric habits of speech. (His extravagant formulations – 'An indiscriminate exacerbation much to be inveighed against meticulously', *DA* 86 – are among the novel's surest touches.) In one scene, the sergeant voices a re-edited version of the 'atomic theory' of *The Third Policeman*, in which people gradually turn into their bicycles, with the essentials taken verbatim from the earlier work (*DA* 73–83). Of course O'Nolan had long given up on publishing the earlier novel: it is not his fault that the recycling is so obvious to us. Even had *The Third Policeman* never appeared, however, Fottrell's obsession with bicycles would seem oddly detached from the rest of *The Dalkey Archive*, in which Mick never gets round to retrieving

80

his own bicycle from the police station. More flagrant still is O'Nolan's reuse of a descriptive passage from the earlier work, spatchcocked in with comical disregard for differences of style and context (*DA* 77–8). Here for the last time, perhaps, is the leader of the 'Ready-Made School' at work. 'The modern novel should be largely a work of reference' (*AS* 25): the twist is that O'Nolan's reference library now includes his own past. This suggests part of the meaning of the otherwise unexplained title: the novel is indeed an 'archive' into which pre-existing ideas and materials have been filed.

The book does make one notable break with the earlier fiction. Late in the writing process, O'Nolan decided to recast in the third person a text that had featured a first-person narrator. The primary intention was to set the reader, and indeed the author, at more distance from the protagonist, Mick Shaughnessy. 'This character is a conceited prig', he explained in a letter, 'and a change to the third person would materially change, so to speak, the camera angle, and facilitate the job of making him more revolting'.[13] 'Revolting' does not seem the right word. What does happen is that Mick's self-esteem rises as the plot progresses, to the point where we read that 'his own function and standing had risen remarkably. ... Clearly enough this task had been assigned to him by Almighty God, and this gave him somewhat the status of priest' (*DA* 134). The conceit is extraordinary, and critics (*FOB* 316) have plausibly found in Mick a sly rewrite of Joyce's Stephen Dedalus – a figure alternately pious and proud, who concludes *A Portrait of the Artist as a Young Man* as a self-styled 'priest of eternal imagination', about to forge 'the uncreated conscience of my race'.[14] But Joyce's attitude to his own character has been notoriously difficult to discern, and what Wayne Booth has called 'the problem of distance' in the *Portrait* recurs in less exalted form in *The Dalkey Archive*.[15] Despite the evidence of O'Nolan's letters – evidence made less emphatic by the fact that he was privately scathing about his other protagonists too – there is little clue in the text itself that we should regard Mick with more suspicion than sympathy. His growing sense of importance indeed has a ridiculous flavour; but the context of the novel makes Mick's pomposity less clear-cut, in two ways. One is that the story is even more absurd than Mick's feelings

81

about it – perhaps, indeed, he is entitled to be self-congratulatory, being in the midst of a campaign to save the world? The second problem is the literary unevenness which repeatedly makes it difficult to know how to interpret the tone of a given passage. O'Nolan's third-person narrator, rather than holding Mick at a distance which would enable condemnation and laughter, wavers between tones, to unpredictable effect. And it is strongly centred on the character of Mick, making it difficult to find a position in the novel which is confidently beyond him.

So the use of the third person does not get O'Nolan far beyond the uninspired first-person narration of Finbarr. Instead it leaves *The Dalkey Archive* with a sheepishly uncertain prose. A self-satisfied passage like the following might be taken as ironic:

> If he had a weakness all his own, it was thoughtless indulgence in alcohol; this dulled moral insight, unbalanced the judgement and – heavens! – could lead the mind to sinful reveries of the carnal kind. With God's help alcohol would soon be put in its place, but not in any sudden silly peremptory gesture. A modulation – adult, urbane, unhurried – was called for. (*DA* 60)

The knowledge of O'Nolan's own professed intention to diminish his protagonist might help us to decide that this is mockery – that Mick's fastidious, pious sense of himself is a target. But this is problematic. For one thing, so much of the book is taken up with Mick's own recall of the plot so far, and his plans for the future, that it seems perverse to make all of these an occasion for mockery. Mick is the vehicle of the narrative, and the author – unlike Sergeant Fottrell with Policeman Pluck's bicycle – is not in a position to give him repeated punctures. In any case, what is to be gained from undermining a figure who has little distinction to begin with? As Sue Asbee notes, Mick's greatest feature is his ordinariness:[16] he is a relatively colourless figure, never described physically by the novel. It is hard to feel that as much is at stake in the treatment of his character as in Joyce's depiction of Stephen Dedalus. Yet there may still be a parallel here. As Anthony Cronin has suggested, Mick may have begun as a highly autobiographical figure, preoccupied with the same questions that were vexing Brian O'Nolan in the late 1940s, 'when it was beginning to be obvious to him that he had a drink problem of a major kind and he was wondering if he could or should ever embark on a serious relationship with a woman' (*NLM* 229). To read O'Nolan's hostility to Mick as repudiating a version of himself – one presented with a greater openness than in his previous fiction – at least offers some motive for the author's vitriol against his character.

It is difficult to locate a point in the novel safely prior to, or beyond, the uncertain prose in which it represents Mick's thoughts. The tone of the passage quoted above is also detectable on the first page, before Mick has even appeared:

> Dalkey looks like an humble settlement which must, a traveller feels, be next door to some place of the first importance and distinction. And it is – vestibule of a heavenly conspection.
> Behold it. Ascend a shaded, dull, lane-like way, *per iter*, as it were, *tenebricosum*, and see it burst upon you as if a curtain had been miraculously whisked away. Yes, the Vico Road.
> Good Lord! (*DA* 7)

A generous reading can find here the most reflexive moments of the novel.[17] The teasingly obtrusive narrator, guiding the reader toward the scene of the action, hams it up with the hey-presto image of a curtain whisked away. A little further down the page the effect continues with a self-conscious parade of alliterative adjectives, prompting the reflection: 'Heavens, has something escaped from the lexicon of Sergeant Fottrell?' (*DA* 7). That is: has the idiom of a character somehow got mixed up with that of the third-person narrator? This is as textually playful as the book gets – but note that its camp ejaculations are echoed in the later passage's 'heavens!' as a reaction to the hint of 'sinful reveries of the carnal kind' (*DA* 60). There is no clear border between narratorial play and the description of Mick's plans: no sense that the coy joshing of the novel's opening is altogether discarded. Instead a residue of the initial friskiness lingers through the whole book, as O'Nolan seems unsure whether to leave it behind or embrace it. The narrator in chapter 2 wonders whether De Selby is 'a theopneust, a geodetic chemist' (*DA* 11); two chapters on it is reflecting that the day 'had been surely one of manicoloured travail', featuring 'acerb disputation' between De Selby and Augustine (*DA* 49). Towards the novel's end James Joyce says he has never heard of gin, and the narrator indulges himself in a serious contender for the worst joke of O'Nolan's career: 'Perhaps Geneva would have been a better name' (*DA* 179). The prose manifests a submerged desire to be manicoloured – but these isolated bursts of flair give the impression of someone who turns up to an ordinary party in fancy dress. At times the writing indeed seems to become embarrassed – and it is no accident that an exemplary instance occurs when O'Nolan tries to describe Mary:

> Mary was no sweetie-pie nor was she pretty but (to Mick's eyes at least) she was good-looking and dignified. Brown-eyed, her personality was russet and usually she was quiet and recollected. He was, he thought, very fond of her and did not by any means regard her as merely a member of her sex, or anything so commonplace and trivial. She was a true obsession with him (he suspected) and kept coming into his head on all sorts of irrelevant occasions without, so to speak, knocking. (*DA* 52)

It is hard to be quite sure whether this is genuinely awkward, or the sort of extended parody of awkwardness that Joyce essayed in the 'Eumaeus' episode of *Ulysses*. 'Sweetie-pie' is a formula disavowed, subtly rejected (it's convenient that Mary is *not* one of these), but 'good-looking and dignified' are not very promising adjectives if we are hoping for vivid description. Myles na gCopaleen, O'Nolan's newspaper alter ego, enjoyed picking at small errors: he would have made mincemeat of the second sentence, with its grammatical implication that Mary's *personality* is brown-eyed. Then there are the shy shuffles of doubt: the two parentheses, like 'he thought' in the third line, withdraw large claims and turn them into subjective suggestions, Mick's guesses at his own feelings. If this manages to be subtly mimetic of the character's hesitancy, that is surely because it also records the author's. It would be a great pastiche of male awkwardness – if it were a pastiche.

Not that such writing is deadly earnest either. It has traces of both straightness and parody: it is anxious not to be taken seriously, but nor is it comic. Like most of the novel's prose, it floats in the space of a slack middle term between comedy and seriousness: *lightness*. This uncertain, unfunny joviality, the element in which Flann O'Brien concludes his career, is marked by two recurring signs of weakness. One is a tendency to recap the narrative, which reaches its peak in recounting Mick's nine-point plan to save the world (*DA* 110–11). At these moments, it is as though O'Nolan has let his notes for the novel spill into the typescript itself – or as though the novel is recounting itself with the deliberate contrivance of *At Swim*'s synopses 'FOR THE BENEFIT OF NEW READERS' (*AS* 60). As with *The Hard Life*, there is a fine line between a badly written novel and an anti-novel: the botched storytelling of *The Dalkey Archive* continually threatens to topple over into an accidental metafiction. This is true, too, of the other recurring oddity: the narrator's tendency to apologize for or undercut his own words. In an echo of Finbarr's reaction to Manus's letters, a conversation on taxation (a subject dear to the later O'Nolan's heart: *NLM* 238) is swiftly dismissed by the news that '[Mick] found the talk arid and useless' (*DA* 122). More strikingly, a motif of the novel is the difficulty of literary representation: 'It is not easy to give an account of the Colza Hotel' (*DA* 25); 'Thinking about the séance (if that ill-used word will serve)' (*DA* 44); 'It is not easy to outline [Sergeant Fottrell's] personal portrait' (*DA* 46); 'Mary was not a simple girl, nor an easy subject to write about' (*DA* 52); 'That account of their chat is not accurate' (*DA* 56); 'It is hard to say why he hated others to hear his meaningless responses' (*DA* 58); 'The town of Skerries has been referred to on another page but it is not easy to convey the air and style of the place' (*DA* 117); 'Mick felt neutralized, if that phrase makes sense' (*DA* 191).

The recurrence of this trait is so marked that it may complicate our sense of the narrator, who emerges from these examples as a modest conversationalist, an obtrusive storyteller apologetic for his struggle with language. We may judge that Thomas F. Shea has a point in his reading of *The Dalkey Archive* as self-conscious literary parody.[18] But the regular undercutting is also the work of a writer who repeatedly redrafted his novel, and repeatedly expressed apologetic surprise at how poor it remained. O'Nolan's sadly self-abasing letter to Tim O'Keeffe, as late as January 1964 – expressing disbelief at 'a farrago of mis-writing, slop, mistypes, repetition, with many passages meaningless' (*NLM* 231) – shows that he remained capable of seeing his own failings. But he was not, at this late stage, able to overcome them on this scale. If *The Dalkey Archive* hints at becoming a self-conscious novel, that must partly be because its author was self-conscious about his waning ability to write a novel.

At least, in doing so, he managed his fullest mockery of the abilities of his great predecessor. Joyce had always been problem as well as solution, obstruction as well as exemplar. In return, O'Nolan had already imagined him as a man locked overnight in a railway carriage toilet (*SP* 169–75). *The Dalkey Archive* reverses that emphasis: Joyce is no longer the carousing rebel but the pious conformist, despised as a 'holy Mary Ann' by his countrymen (*DA* 128). The flight hymned by the *Portrait* is likewise inverted: the goal of this Joyce has not been to fly by the nets but to land safely beneath them, to escape chaotic Europe and recover stable Ireland. This is the revenge of a man who lived in a suburban bungalow.[19] There are traces of respect: the terms of Mick's praise for Joyce's work (*DA* 96) echo O'Nolan's own, and he insisted that his aim was to mock the US-based Joyce Industry rather than the man himself.[20] Indeed, the encounters with Joyce deliberately go into biographical detail to display the author's knowledge of his life and work. But this can heighten the insult, as in the final indignity – Joyce's prospective job repairing the Jesuits' underwear – which echoes not only Joyce's schooling but his interest in other kinds of underwear. Joyce, O'Nolan admitted, had been 'dragged in by the scruff of the neck' (*NLM* 230). Perhaps the opportunity to do that, just this once, was enough.

6

Local Unaesthetic: *Cruiskeen Lawn*

Flann O'Brien was a failure, and Myles na Gopaleen was to blame. This has become a critical consensus. '[A] disappointed man, even, strange paradox, a disappointed writer', writes Anthony Cronin (*NLM* vii). Declan Kiberd wanly judges that 'his real potential, as thinker and as artist, may never have been suspected, and was surely not realized'.[1] And there is agreement on the roots of this failure. Drink may have shortened his life; journalism sapped his art. 'For twenty-five years', laments Hugh Kenner, 'the columns used him up'.[2] Seamus Deane accepts as fact O'Nolan's 'failure' and names 'the demands of his thrice-weekly column' as one cause.[3] For Bernard Benstock, 'the twenty-year suppression of the talented Flann by the irrepressible Myles' smothers O'Brien's career as surely as death ended that of Joyce.[4] 'The cost was massive', writes Kiberd, who mourns 'the immense talent wasted in the service of [the *Irish Times* editor] R. M. Smyllie'.[5]

The list could go on: the consensus is clear. There is much sense in it. The structure of O'Nolan's career is extraordinary: his early flowering as a novelist, writing three major works in quick succession, is followed by two decades in exile from the genre. In this period the *Irish Times* indeed claims most of his ideas and energy: yet the late return to fiction suggests that the desire to be a novelist has endured. *Cruiskeen Lawn* indeed looks like the problem: a distraction from the real business of writing, a diversion of artistic energy into mere ephemera. We can accept the important truth contained in this reading. O'Nolan himself surely did, as the increasing bitterness of his later years suggests.

Yet the story falls down in one crucial respect. It fails to register the achievement of *Cruiskeen Lawn* – fails to notice what all that wasted talent actually generated, rather than what it didn't. What if, rather than viewing the column as a hindrance to O'Nolan's creativity, we should regard it as an outlet in which his peculiar talent thrived? What if O'Nolan's major work, far from being prevented by the column, was in plain view all along, in the pages of the *Irish Times*? Recently, some critics have begun thinking along these lines. 'We critics', observes Steven Young, 'have no category for the artist who transforms the banal into art, but insists on leaving it in the realm of the ephemeral and the topical. *Cruiskeen Lawn* has not received the attention it deserves, because it runs counter to our available ways of talking about literature.'[6] On such a basis, John Wyse Jackson makes a strong case for the journalism, as 'one of the great monuments of the century, a modernist (or rather a proleptically postmodernist) *coup de maître*, written in two primary and several secondary languages whose boundaries are repeatedly fused'. He bids us think of *Cruiskeen Lawn* as 'some unidentified subspecies of the fiction family, a random, episodic, wildly innovative rough beast of a "novel", in which the novel form itself has been stretched to screaming point and beyond' (*AW* 11).

Jackson's final qualification is important. There is no point in trying to make *Cruiskeen Lawn* fit into a reassuring model of fiction beyond which it has already broken. To say with Steven Young that the column is 'a new kind of novel'[7] is most useful not as a bid for firm classification but as a gesture of estrangement, which makes us rethink the relation between different genres of writing. Certainly *Cruiskeen Lawn*, in its fantastical and yarn-spinning dimensions, is a kind of fiction, whatever else it might be. 'I am not begging the question in calling [it] a "novel" ', wrote T. S. Eliot of *Ulysses*, 'and if you call it an epic it will not matter'.[8] We do call *Ulysses* a novel, provisionally and for want of some other word. Whether we call *Cruiskeen Lawn* a new kind of novel will not much matter, as long as we can find the terms with which to appreciate it. This chapter aims to provide some of those terms, and to encourage readers to produce their own.

MYLES' STYLES

Cruiskeen Lawn was Brian O'Nolan's way of announcing his views to the world; but to an important degree, the column also maintained, or increased, his tendency toward masks and evasion. 'Myles na gCopaleen' is crucial here.

The name derived, characteristically, from literature. Myles na gCopaleen had appeared first in Gerald Griffin's *The Collegians* (1829), and again in Dion Boucicault's popular play *The Colleen Bawn* (1860), in which he sings the song 'Cruiskeen Lawn'. The name means 'Myles of the Ponies' or 'Myles of the Little Horses'; translations vary on this just as they do on *Cruiskeen Lawn* itself, which veers from 'The Full Little Jug of Ale' to 'The Overflowing Little Jug' (*AW* 13). The original Myles is a genial figure, a horse-dealer and drinker, and, as Anne Clissmann notes, 'a good story-teller who can make a simple incident into a strange and vivid story' (*FOB* 191). Boucicault's play emphasized his comic dimensions, bringing him closer to the type of the stage Irishman. Declan Kiberd sees a political significance in O'Nolan's reclamation of this figure: 'The feckless clown who had once stuttered in broken English is now permitted to speak in his native language, and so he is shown not as the English wish to visualize him, but as he sees himself'.[9] He also finds the altered spellings of the character's names significant. Boucicault's man had been 'na Coppaleen'; O'Nolan began as na gCopaleen, then gradually became na Gopaleen. The change, Jack White recalls, was made for the benefit of readers without Irish.[10] Kiberd views the blunting of 'gC' into the cruder, Anglo-friendly 'G' as a deliberate mistranslation: 'as if, by this alteration, O'Nolan wished to indicate a loss of authenticity'.[11] Perhaps; but as we shall see, O'Nolan was also keen on maximizing his readership, and the simpler name may have reflected his desire for commercial success and international recognition.[12]

Pointed as the choice of name may have been, the figure of Myles diverged from his literary predecessor, becoming a notable character in his own right. But 'character' is hardly the word. O'Nolan undoubtedly made Myles up as he went along: the figure's extensive life-stories were no more in his head, to begin with, than the unpredictable responses to the Ibsen debate had been. Myles is not so much a conventional persona, more an ongoing improvisation, who (or 'which') picks up voices and backgrounds as he ('it') goes. Anne Clissmann notes some of them:

> He was a multiplicity of characters – at once a Dublin 'gutty', a famous journalist, an art critic, banker, archaeologist, inhabitant of Santry, aesthete, civil servant, social commentator, and anything else he wanted to be according to the dictates of his mood or as a likely subject for satire or parody presented itself. (*FOB* 192)

Myles, that's to say, is a function of style. As a 'character' he is a deliberate impossibility: he takes one form after another, and his origins shift as he progresses. He has something in common with the flickering figures in Joyce's *Finnegans Wake*, shape-changers who blend in and out of one another and occupy different historical moments simultaneously; more locally, he descends from the diverse role-playing of O'Nolan's own Brother Barnabas. 'Each of his biographies', Clissmann adds,

> is different from its predecessor, though *in toto* they provide an unparalleled illustration of the great man's talents and importance. His readers neither expected, nor received, a coherent narrative. Myles . . . transcended time, space and continuity – all the human limitations. (*FOB* 193)

Clissmann rightly suggests that part of the function of Myles is not to be a coherent character, but to offer a principle of continuity for the column (*FOB* 190). Disparate materials are notionally unified by the attachment of his name.

The primary character of *Cruiskeen Lawn* is no stage Irishman. The column's predominant voice is cool, crisp, sardonic. It depends heavily on irony, and a frequent note of exasperation:

> Assuming that to 'write' is mechanically to multiply communication (sometimes a very strong assumption, particularly when one writes a book about peasants in Irish) what vast yeasty eructation of egotism drives a man to address simultaneously a mass of people he has never met and who may resent being pestered with his 'thoughts'? (*BM* 237)

This is characteristic: irritation, manifested in eloquence and precision (the pedantry of the opening definition, the lengthy, dismissive parenthesis; the outlandish deliberateness of 'vast yeasty eructation of egotism'). Crucial is the effect of superiority: the voice's ability to stand above what it scorns, the better slowly to dissect it. In one sense its deployment of eloquence is typical of an Irish tradition; but it spurns artificial local colour. The tone is devoid of shamrock and sentiment, and deadly in its clear-eyed scorn.

A still grander kind of superiority appears periodically, in Myles na gCopaleen's accounts of his life as a universal statesman. Here he complains that the powers dividing Europe at the war's end have not consulted him:

> Readers will join me in offering My Excellency heartfelt condolences on the recent occurrences. . . . During my absence, during the short disinhabitation of the rostrum whereon resides my absolute authority, during my most voluntary immurement within Melleray, events base and felonious, terrible in their enchargement with vanity and folly, were suffered to occur. (*AW* 171)

This brand of play is recurrent. Myles lays claim to vast authority, and either revels in it or expresses disbelief at the insolent obliviousness of the rest of the world. 'Myles na gCopaleen' becomes a fantasy of power: a means, perhaps – for all its manifest absurdity – by which O'Nolan imaginatively arrogates to himself the influence he lacks in reality. The civil servant, embittered by the folly and avarice he claims to see in his day job, takes fantastic revenge. In the pages of the *Irish Times* he can rule Ireland, the job which he – but only he, alas – knows he deserves. As Anthony Cronin recalls, both O'Nolan and Patrick Kavanagh had a 'proprietorial' relationship with Ireland, a claim 'to be asserted against politicians and other usurpers':

> No doubt this could be described, in some of its manifestations anyway, as a form of megalomania. It might also be thought to be something both men had derived, in however inchoate a way, from their bardic forebears. (*NLM* 191–2)

The bardic impulse is indeed reinvented in the figure of Myles na gCopaleen, the scribe who dominates a fantasy Ireland.

Yet the column also derives its material from the real Ireland around it: above all from its voices, overheard and rewritten.

Late in life O'Nolan told an interviewer that he had 'made a bit of a fetish of the natural way of speaking in Dublin', a speech too often 'botched' by writers who 'don't know how to listen'. The feature he most admired in James Joyce, he often said, was his ear: his capacity to render a Dublin speech that had previously been absent from literature (*NLM* 247). This is also a central feature of *Cruiskeen Lawn*. It can turn up as part of Myles' own persona. The column's 'base language', its primary dialect, is the crisp Standard English we have just witnessed: but this is always liable to mutate into a more distinctively Dublin voice. Sometime the addition of individual words indicates a kind of linguistic blurring: 'that crowd', 'that class', 'me' (for 'my'), 'meself'. At times the Dublin words appear in parentheses, as though Myles is only hinting at the dialect voice he could launch if he wished: 'Rather curious thing happened to me (there) the other day' (*BM* 173); 'I see (where) Sir Bernard Shaw has been writing letters to the papers' (*BM* 244). Here, more extensively, a meditation on the ambiguity of newspaper headlines, which has proceeded with Myles' characteristic elaborate precision, suddenly flicks into another dialect:

> Ah well! Need I say that when I read POST-WAR COPPER PROBLEMS, I immediately refused to admit two 'meanings'. Number wan was the possibility that some of the cute lads in Justice were getting out sketch-plans for . . . brain-new stainless arterial polismen, made of plastic material and 100 per cent prefabricated, to be laid on with th'elechtric and the wather afther the waaaar.   (*BM* 373)

Standard English here flips unannounced into the dialogue of Sean O'Casey. Such linguistic variation makes Myles a less stable and predictable voice: he floats as freely between the dialects as between English, Irish and Latin. It is a performance, a bravura demonstration of his literary capacity. But the slide into Dublin dialect differs from the use of other European languages, in its implication of the local. It's a means of winking at the readership – or better, of suddenly mimicking the imagined reader, disconcertingly and sarcastically closing the gap between the sage and his audience.

Myles never demonstrates his mastery of local speech more memorably than in the columns concerning 'the Brother'. For all the weight that his name carries in the Myles canon, the Brother never actually appears: like Beckett's Godot, he is an absent centre around whom others generate talk. Myles' long-suffering monologue is displaced by a dialogue between two voices: the Dubliner who speaks in O'Nolan's finely wrought version of local dialect, and the impersonal voice of fastidious Standard English. 'The Brother has it all worked out', the Dubliner announces in an early column: 'The war. How we can get through the war here in the Free State. I mean the rationing and brown bread and all that class of thing' (*BM* 46). The plan is for everyone in Ireland to go to bed for a week every month:

> *That strikes me as a curious solution to difficulties in this dynamic iron age.*
>
> D'ye see, when nobody is up you save clothes, shoes, rubber, petrol, coal, turf, timber and everything we're short of. And food, too, remember. Because tell me this – what makes you hungry? It's work that makes you hungry. Work and walking around and swallying pints and chawin' the rag at the street corner. Stop in bed an' all you'll ask for is an odd slice of bread. . . . If nobody's up, there's no need for anybody to do any work because everybody in the world does be workin' for everybody else.
>
> *I see. In a year therefore you would effect a saving of twenty-five per cent in the consumption of essential commodities.*
>
> Well now I don't know about that, but you'd save a quarter of everything, and that would be enough to see us right.   (*BM* 46–7)

Myles plays two voices off against each other: the idiosyncrasies of the plain man and the rationalistic dryness of the bureaucrat. It is an encounter between two exaggerations. One voice, we could say, needs to be spoken, while the one in italics can only be written. One figure is all local colour, the other black and white: one voice overflows with a sense of presence, the other figure is almost impossible to envisage.

Yet there is a kind of inversion here, for it is the man in the street who goes beyond common sense. The Brother's idea is Mylesian in its seemingly irrefutable logic: it's true that if we all simultaneously refrained from doing anything, we would need less energy than usual. The refutation of this piece of reasoning lies outside its own internally coherent terms. As in much of O'Nolan's work, the Brother's notions start from what seems rational and somehow become absurd. It is worth noting, though, that the Brother columns broach this absurdity in historically specific ways. In the column quoted above, this weird rationality is explicitly specific to the war. This is not bad logic so much as Emergency logic: and perhaps that can be said for much of *Cruiskeen Lawn*. The column began as an eccentric antidote to the actual in a precariously neutral country. While it managed to outlive the war by twenty years, there is much agreement that its brand of nonsense never made more sense than in the first half of the 1940s. Oscar Love, of all people, responded to the advent of the column by recognizing that its 'nonsense' was a 'new sense' which might be salutary in a world of dictators (*FOB* 187).

The encounter between the two voices of the Brother columns vividly stages an encounter between the local and the universal – between 'Ireland' and a generalized rationality which transcends it. In play here is a regular Mylesian concern: the relation between Ireland and the rest of the world. The very first column had turned, obliquely, on the place of neutral Ireland in a world at war, wondering whether a nation devoted to the revival of the Irish language could keep pace with modern concepts and military terminology (*FC* 13–15). Myles' comic solution, which provoked the ire of the Gaelic League (*FOB* 184–7), had been an ingenious series of translations of the phrase 'Molotoff Bread-Basket' (*FC* 14). In a less drastic way, the 'Brother' scenario also poses questions of translation: it turns on the comic incompatibility between the voice of Dublin and the voice of reason. This is also, perhaps, a division within Brian O'Nolan himself, between the hard-drinking humorist and the bean-counting civil servant. But the gap is not absolute: and the obsessive rationalist Myles does not hold his Dubliner in contempt. As in *At Swim-Two-Birds*, there is a delight here in the idiosyncrasies of the daily speech around him, which the column has unwittingly recorded for posterity. And as Anthony Cronin astutely remarks, O'Nolan's written dialect is as much an invention as a record.[13] Myles complains that Synge – who's mistakenly considered 'a bit of a genius, indeed, like the brother' – has influenced real speech: 'I have personally met in the streets of Ireland people who are clearly out of Synge's plays' (*BM* 235). But in forging the brother of the Brother, he may have had an analogous effect on his own audience.

Cruiskeen Lawn endlessly plays with that audience: conspiring and confiding at one moment, haughtily dismissing the next. Myles' Irishness is unmistakable – save that he will address the readers as 'You Irish', a people whose foibles he fails to understand (*AW* 146, *FOB* 213). Most flagrantly, he includes a version of the audience in the column itself, as the Plain People of Ireland (PPI). The PPI are a principle of interruption: they force (that is, allow) Myles to abandon his pedantic monologue and enter into exasperated dialogue. The contrast hones the learned and superior aspects of his persona, for the PPI are gullible, unsophisticated, in almost touching need of guidance. When one of Myles' pseudo-legal discourses incongruously mentions 'fishing smacks', they suddenly intervene:

> *The Plain People of Ireland:* Where do the fishing smacks come in?
> *Myself:* Howth, usually.
> *The Plain People of Ireland:* No, but what have they got to do with what you were saying?
> *Myself:* It's all right. I was only trying to find out whether ye were still reading on. By the way, I came across something very funny the other night in a public-house.
> *PPI (chuckling):* What was it?
> *Myself:* It was a notice on the wall. It read: 'We have come to an arrangement with our bankers. They have agreed not to sell drink. We, on our part, have agreed not to cash cheques'.
> *PPI:* O, Ha Ha Ha! Ho Ho Ho! (*Sounds of thousands of thighs being slapped in paroxysms of mirth.*)
> *Myself:* Good. I knew that would amuse you.   (*BM* 85)

A discrepancy is implied between writer and reader: Myles' last line here signals his disdainful recognition that the PPI's sense of humour does not match his own. Here as elsewhere, at their request, he replaces elaborate themes with Christmas-cracker jokes (*BM* 97), parodies of Hollywood cinema and potboiler fiction (*BM* 95, 108–10), and verbal puzzles at which the admiring PPI declare, 'O it's very hard to be up to you be times, especially the days when you do have jawbreakers in the paper' (*BM* 96).

The whole thing is an allegory of author and audience, a means for O'Nolan not only to imagine his readership's response but to generate mocking copy out of it. But its implications should not be taken too literally. Hugh Kenner reads the PPI columns as a dramatization of O'Nolan's despair at the philistinism of the readers for whom he was condemned to write.[14] Uncharacteristically, Kenner misses the irony involved. In at least three ways, the PPI columns are more complex than they look.

Firstly, Myles himself, as we shall see, is a kind of philistine. The PPI's befuddled response to Myles' description of a painter – 'It's very hard to be up to you intellectual lads' (*BM* 89) – spares him the energy of his own attack on the 'corduroys'. To that degree the PPI are a displaced version of O'Nolan, as much as his antagonists.

Secondly: the PPI are ordinary folk, mistrustful of difficulty and formal experiment. But their appearance actually facilitates some of O'Nolan's most daring play with the form of the column. Interruption, fragmentation, self-referentiality – those tendencies of *At Swim* are here in a new form, in the dialogues between author and readers. Unlike some of Myles' other Dublin dialogues, these exchanges are not just the 'content' of the column: the conceit is that they're between its 'inside' (Myles) and its 'outside' (the reader). They're about the column (they are a debate about the appropriateness of its contents) but they're also part of it (they are its contents). This is an impossibility, with which the deftness of the writing prevents us from bothering. More cutely still, the dialogue sometimes concerns the actual layout on the newspaper: when Myles is interrupted by giddiness, the PPI advise him that 'You're too high up. No oxygen. . . . Come on down lower in the page and you'll be game ball' (*BM* 102). In short, the appearance of the timid and uncomprehending audience is actually the occasion for textual play of a sort never essayed by Flann O'Brien.

Thirdly, the PPI are not the real audience – they are an object for the amusement of the real audience. Their appearance thus flatters the readers as much as it chides them: only if Myles' readers are more sophisticated than the PPI can they laugh at the PPI. The overall effect is a mixture of satire (mockery of the putative real-world equivalents of the PPI, who are by defini-

tion *not* the right audience for *Cruiskeen Lawn*), reader-friendli-
ness (the inclusion of even this benighted audience-figure
helps to draw in and orient the audience), and warning (the
actual readership is advised not to react as foolishly as the
PPI). So the device is ambiguous: if it appears to register
despair at an uncomprehending country, it also implies a class
of sophisticates to share the despair.

THE CLICHÉ EMERGENCY

Few instalments of *Cruiskeen Lawn* go by without Myles'
distinctive word-play. His prose, as it goes about its polemical
business, is frequently pulled sideways into a systematic series
of puns or verbal quivers which can seem to take over the text:

> I am, as you know, an Irish person and I yield to gnomon in my
> admiration and respect for the old land.   (*AW* 109)

And more outlandishly,

> I was the most inveterate smoker in the you and I, Ted King
> (dumb).   (*AW* 110)

This is partly the writer enjoying himself, the self-styled hack
making his own typewriting life more interesting. But it also
alters the reader's experience of the column: makes it into a
text which, rather than proceeding progressively through an
argument, is liable at any moment to move off in another
direction, driven purely by the sound of words. An unpredictable, non-logical force is at work in the writing: we are taught
to be alive to what words are doing, because what they're
doing is not what the argument is doing. (The subterranean
principle of the pun is brought above ground in the 'Keats and
Chapman' pieces, where the pun becomes the unabashed aim
of the text rather than a decorative extra.)

A variant on the pun is the deliberate typo or printing error,
which can become pointed:

> Talking still of the abombic tomb – I *meant* atomic bomb but leave
> it, I am a neutron in such matters.   (*AW* 173)

Here we are closer to the puns of *Finnegans Wake*, in which
aural or visual proximities hint at thematic ones: the tricks of

language become a means of lateral thinking. It would be wrong to consider Myles' verbal antics as 'mere' play: they involve a work of thought too. Typically, the focus is on that form which yielded Myles so much material: the cliché. Four textual tactics can be observed here: parenthesis, paraphrase, catechism, and inversion.

Here is an example of the first:

> Perfect agreement was reached on many points and it was felt that the relationship between the two countries had (much to gain) (from this frank exchange of views). It had been intended also to exchange notes but owing (to pressure of time) it was only found possible to exchange views.
> . . . .
>
> Who this person was and what we talked about, of course, I am (not in a position to disclose). A (prominent spokesman) would probably call what we were doing (intense diplomatic activity). (*BM* 218)

It ought to be possible to remove the parentheses from a sentence, with no loss of coherence. But the bracketed material here cannot actually be lost. In one sense the parentheses mark the boundaries of a cliché: it's as though they are the physical index of the typesetter's tools, within which the prefabricated phrase is kept ready for use. In another sense the brackets work to mark the writer's distance from the cliché. The formula is shuffled into the sentence with embarrassment, half-hidden behind its brackets: the parentheses are the way that the rest of the sentence shields its eyes from such barbarisms. They suggest a space which ought to be filled, if possible, with something else: the cliché is doing duty between them, the only phrase available to the hack at the time of writing. The cliché is thus provisional, yet threatens to linger for ever: it's an embarrassment, but can't quite be discarded. In one dystopian paragraph, cliché has taken over taken over entirely: every phrase is parenthetical (*BM* 316).

A second manoeuvre is the paraphrase. Here Myles leaves behind the introduction to a column:

> That was only by way of that obscure instrument that performs what seems to be an absolutely unnecessary task – a pipe-opener. Today I am occupied with a well-known alternative culinary operation, I have other fish to fry. (*AW* 88)

Or more elaborately, he is refused an audience with his editor:

> Am I that arithmetical symbol of no value in itself but multiplying the number it is placed after, and dividing the decimal number it is placed before, by ten – a mere cipher? (*AW* 87)

Central to the joke here is the extra effort involved. Myles writes not just the cliché but an alternative version of it, and his sentences can become inordinately long and intricate as a result. The phrasing must be spot-on to set up the cliché which is imminent, but its excess makes a mockery of the cliché – for the whole point of a cliché is to save time and effort. The cliché is a device for saving semantic labour: but Myles' paraphrase of them actually costs him far more words and energy than are needed. The joke is thus founded on an imbalance: and this signals a deeper imbalance, the lack of real fit between cliché and world. The weirdness of the paraphrase is only rectified by the arrival of the cliché, which ends a sentence by guiding us back to the conversational norm. But insofar as the paraphrase accurately matches the content of the cliché, it starkly reminds us of the phrase's radical inappropriateness in this context. The paraphrase reminds us of what the cliché literally means: and what it literally means is askew to its use. 'A cliché', writes Myles, 'is a phrase that has become fossilised, its component words deprived of their intrinsic light and meaning by incessant usage' (*BM* 227).

Incessant usage is an occupational hazard for useful words, and attacks on cliché should be phrased with caution. Phrases are not content to remain literal, and ready-made formulas are part of communication. But metaphors have a way of dying, and clogging up the tongue with their corpses. Myles' verbal intricacies remind us that words are what we think with, and the anguish with which he confronts cliché is also a lament for the ossification of thought. But in highlighting a cliché's metaphorical character, Myles actually re-energizes it, restores the figurative power that resides in its distance from what it denotes. The energy thus injected might just be what's needed to propel the cliché out of the way.

Myles himself is rarely more energetic than in his composition of the Myles na gCopaleen Catechism of Cliché:

– In what can no man tell the future has for us?
– Store.
– With what do certain belligerents make their military disposi-
tions?
– Typical Teutonic thoroughness.
– In what manner do wishful thinkers imagine that the war will be
over this year?
– Fondly.
– Take the word, 'relegate'. To what must a person be relegated?
– That obscurity from which he should never have been permitted
to emerge.
– What may one do with a guess, provided one is permitted?
– Hazard.
– And what is comment?
– Superfluous.   (*BM* 206)

The Catechism is characteristic of O'Nolan, in its rationalistic
pursuit of the logic of something that does not deserve to be
treated so logically. The most banal locutions Myles can find
are solemnly treated not as isolated infelicities but as a
connected system, a coherent pattern of discursive pain, a
whole verbal universe of lucky stars and blue moons. An
alternative intellectual world becomes founded on error or
poverty of imagination. Yet, while the painstaking wildness of
de Selby in *The Third Policeman* can be passed off as a flight of
fancy, the Catechism of Cliché is closer to home. The point is
that all its materials are recognizable – more than that, are
overly recognizable, are by definition more than recognizable,
are precisely the kind of sentences one is most likely to employ
should one pluck up the self-importance to write to the *Irish
Times*. The unhappy joke of the Catechism of Cliché is not so
much that we can imagine a world like this, as that this is our
world, day in day out.

The question posed by the Catechism habitually contains the
bulk of the cliché in question, yet in an incomplete state. 'In
what can no man tell the future has for us?' Deceptively, the
question looks not only eccentric but ungrammatical, for the
series of subjects, objects and prepositions which make up the
cliché have been shuffled out of order and into a new format
which is strictly correct but looks like a Martian's attempt at
English. Or perhaps a Teuton's; or even an Irishman's, for as

the Plain People of Ireland say elsewhere in the *Cruiskeen Lawn*, 'Very guttural languages the pair of them the Gaelic and the German' (*BM* 105). A piece of language whose defining quality is its familiarity – its readiness to be picked up as a prefabricated unit, a stereotype block, no less, and stamped in the middle of a faltering sentence – is made momentarily unfamiliar, until the answer arrives to be inserted into the semantic disconcert and make things familiar again. This is also the prime comic moment, when the joke is clarified in its several pleasures: the agonizing ever-readiness of the phrase reassembled by the reader; the gymnastics to which the interrogator has gone to delay its arrival; the discrepancy between the two.

The Catechism of Cliché carries the shadowy suggestion of the cliché of catechism: that the Catholic catechism *is* a cliché, or is about cliché. The omniscience of the real catechist – the infallibility of the body of knowledge at which he probes – is demeaned by comparison with the catechist of cliché, whose stock of stock phrases is equally closed to any questions save those which confirm it. Cliché is a given, a standing army of phrases drilled into automated response; so, the comparison might run, is theology. But the logic of this likeness is no kinder in the other direction. The Catechism of Cliché's more damning implication is not that catechism is cliché, but that cliché is like catechism: that the forms of knowledge and writing to hand in modern Ireland are of a scholastic rigidity which belies their self-image. If catechism is mocked for its resemblance to cliché, the users of cliché are shown to be as predictable as bishops. In this sense the form parodies the intimacy of the religious and the secular enshrined in the Irish Constitution in 1937. At a time when Ireland was insistent on its autonomy and distinctiveness, the Catechism also portrays its English as second-hand and unthinking: a series of mechanical jerks, a stuck record.

With varied methods, then, Myles probes at the limits of public discourse, pointing up ways in which it circumvents rather than enables thought. Yet his work with words can be productive as well as destructive, when he seeks the inverse of a familiar phrase. Here he has narrowly escaped the blast from an exploding apricot:

An attempt on my life? If this means that somebody thinks I should die, I hope somebody else will think it worth while to make an attempt on my death. Because this would surely mean an attempt to prolong my alleged life indefinitely ... (*AW* 93)

The cliché is a means of not thinking: but here it is used as an occasion *for* thinking, as Myles works outwards from a standard form of words to one that we don't have. The phrase 'an attempt on my death' does not exist – but why shouldn't it? The example hints that there is a whole expanse of concepts on the other side of our speech that is silently going unused.

There are sundry other cases like this: referring to 'those quare contradictory men, false pretences', he wonders, 'and who ever heard of true pretences?' (*AW* 86). Who indeed: but their existence would seem to be implied by the false variety; and perhaps the idea of true pretences does describe something anew. In inverting a given cliché, Myles occasionally achieves the reverse of cliché: a metaphor logically arrived at, fresh-minted, prompting new intellectual work rather than impeding it.

THE WORK OF ART IN THE AGE OF MYLES na gCOPALEEN

Cruiskeen Lawn, notes Steven Young, troubles the rules of art. It is artful, possessed of great semantic self-consciousness, wildly imaginative. But it is also fragmentary, frequent, throwaway. 'The column', muses Young, 'may give the reader a passing pleasure over morning coffee, or on the bus to work, but the novels are for the ages. How can it be art one day and be used to wrap fish and chips the next?'[15] But in its way *At Swim-Two-Birds* provoked the same quandary: its roots were in the 'readymade school',[16] its text punctuated with pilferings. O'Nolan's approach to 'art' was subversive from the start: and *Cruiskeen Lawn* may be viewed, not as a retreat from that approach, but as its logical consequence. His first novel made literature out of borrowed texts and parodied voices: the column into which he diverted himself was a more direct realization of this principle. More direct, because of its context – its resituation of all that polyphony and fragmentation into their natural environment, the newspaper. The qualities that distinguish O'Nolan's fiction, writes Young,

> digressiveness, competing voices, the anonymity of the writing, also fit the essential qualities of journalism. The newspaper is itself a cacophony of competing voices with no unifying artistic voice to make them pull together, a mirror of the flux and chaos of daily life.[17]

James Joyce had fashioned a secular sacred book which aimed to contain the world, not least the forms and rhythms of the newspaper.[18] Brian O'Nolan, always in need of a way to trump or evade the master, went the other way, taking the comic intelligence of his great anti-novel into the newspaper itself. It was an ambiguous reverse colonization, in which the literary man might conquer and be conquered: winning a daily audience of proportions undreamt of by W. B. Yeats, yet also, in the opinion of many, throwing his gifts away on hackwork.

Perhaps O'Nolan shared that view. But he was also endlessly sceptical about the very idea of art, not least in *Cruiskeen Lawn* itself. The column is always suspicious of the local bohemians, poets, 'corduroys' as he calls them – 'The writing crowd, it is well known, are only a parcel of dud czechs and bohemian gulls' (*BM* 241) – and he frequently produces mockeries of their speech (*BM* 111, 249; *AW* 33–4, 39). Myles' hostility to art can become a predictable pose, as he flirts with a philistinism so commonplace that it hardly merits enshrining in print. But his particular emphases can add an illuminating perspective on his own writing. What repeatedly emerges is an opposition between art and 'work'.

We can view this clearly in a column which takes to task a new journal, 'PUCK FARE'. Myles begins by noting the value of working men, experts in their trade, for solving problems – a leaking roof, an untuned piano. These honest artisans are compared with the producers of the magazine, which is printed 'on white paper fully glazed and fashioned and dedicated to the nice whimsy that the writer – *the writer*, do you know – is a professional man, a *craft*sman, a highly trained party who should never be paid less than five bar for a good job' (*BM* 231). The burden of Myles' attack is the unworthiness of modern artists to claim the title of 'craftsman'. He begins by taking the claim at face value: 'the layman may be permitted to check admiringly over the shining machinery. Grammar and spelling, I mean – we know it's all right but we'd like to look. The emptor is entitled to demand that his hired literary man be literate at least' (*BM* 232). The strategy of literalization is at work again here. If Irish writers lay claim to craftsmanship, Myles will test the claim, giving their work a once-over.

Unsurprisingly, he finds it malfunctioning, jerry-built from poor materials. With exemplary pedantry Myles lists all the spelling errors he can find, including the parenthetical 'And what's more, "cyclops" is singular' (*BM* 232). The point is to expose the writers as bad workmen, whose superiority to the rest of the population is an illusion. 'Any professional hack would be sacked overnight if he were guilty of the things I have mentioned', Myles concludes: 'The parties responsible may be worth one and six in the writing world but certainly not five bob' (*BM* 233). To bring it down to money is to demystify. These 'literary' men, the attack implies, ought to be paid on a proper scale, which has been displaced by the aura of art. The writer from whom they could learn proper standards is the 'professional hack'. And that, most immediately, suggests Myles na gCopaleen, the jobbing columnist. It is the journalist, not the artist, who is the true 'craftsman' – the expert on whom you can call to fix a leaky paragraph. There is a claim to superiority here, but it is also a defence mechanism against the journalist's sense of inferiority. In exposing the illiteracy of the self-proclaimed artist, the professional hack takes his revenge on literature.

Myles hints at a more complex position in another polemic. From a book on Irish art he quotes a disdainful critic of portraits 'of those people whose highest aim in life or the summit of whose ambition is merely to be captain of the golf club, president of some trade association, chairman of a commercial enterprise, or the wife of one of these' (*BM* 250). He works himself up into a condemnation of this point of view:

But this much I do know – (face gets red and neck bulges) this much I do know – that there is nothing contemptible about being the captain of a golf club or owning a jam factory that makes a lot of money and if the eldest girl now in Eccles Street manages to become the wife of a jam factory, there certainly will be no complaints from yours truly; it will be a little bit more satisfactory than having her mess up bits of canvas as well as her face with 'paints'. Or is it suggested, forsooth, that it is 'easy' to succeed in business? (I can't off-hand think of anything easier than to be an 'artist' in Ireland today – if it be not to be a newspaper funny man.) (*BM* 250)

This balances delicately between polemic and pose. Myles launches into a characteristic tirade against the claims of art, insisting that the value of the 'working' world is not merely equal but greater. Yet he disarmingly undermines himself along the way. The imagined daughter, absurdly pictured marrying a jam factory, ironizes his own case; and in the first parenthesis he openly makes himself into a caricature. Most significant of all is the pay-off. If artists are spongers, those final brackets whisper, what does that make Myles na gCopaleen? As far back as *Blather*, O'Nolan could be seen boosting and denigrating his own work in equally exaggerated measure; Myles' attack on art performs the same oscillation. On one hand he stresses his dignity as a journalist, a man who writes for a broad public and gets paid by the paragraph – in a word, a worker. On the other hand he is willing to let the mask slip, long enough to allow the thought that his column might be an even less substantial kind of work than that of the artists he scorns. For all the polemical lather, Myles has a disarming ability thus to round on himself, suddenly displaying a wry self-knowledge that had seemed unavailable. The battle between art and work is momentarily suspended.

In the background of Myles' whole confrontation with 'art' stands James Joyce, whose example posed a problem for O'Nolan from start to finish. Anthony Cronin records that O'Nolan and his student contemporaries found a reading of Joyce which helped to reduce his challenge to them: 'Joyce and his challenge would be defused by making him a mere logomachic wordsmith, a great but demented genius who finally went mad in his ivory tower. Admittedly he was a great low-life humorist as well, but he was one whose insensate dedication to something called art would finally unhinge him' (*NLM* 52). 'Something called art': that way lay self-indulgence and isolation, the delusions of the solipsist who had turned his back on the ordinary world of work and communication. This view is still evident in O'Nolan's 1951 essay on Joyce, who is envisaged 'innerly locked in the toilet of a locked coach where he has no right to be, resentfully drinking someone else's whiskey, being whisked hither and thither by anonymous shunters, keeping fastidiously the while on the outer face of his door the simple word, ENGAGED' (*SP* 173).

Against this self-exiled figure, O'Nolan sought to imagine a different kind of writer. He would claim as his model the professional scribe: a figure whose hard-headed commercialism prevented any loss of contact with the public. Again and again he discussed writing in terms of money. As Cronin observes, it is telling that O'Nolan sent copies of *At Swim-Two-Birds* not only to Joyce in Paris but also to the popular novelist Ethel Mannin:

> This attempt reveals a curious dichotomy in his outlook. . . . All his life he was to cherish a naïve belief that his works would prove immediately successful, would sell in large quantities and would even perhaps make him a great deal of money; that he would become, like Ethel Mannin and even Margaret Mitchell, a rich, popular author. (*NLM* 94–5)

Gone with the Wind was indeed oddly recurrent in O'Nolan's career. It was the book that *At Swim* had briefly displaced as Dublin's bestselling novel in April 1939 (*FOB* 80). It was a butt of humour in the *Irish Times* debate around Kavanagh: F O'Brien wrote in to say that 'A book that has won for its author many thousands of tons of tubers cannot be dismissed so lightly' (*MBM* 208). That sounds like a mere joke, but six months earlier O'Nolan had said as much in a private letter to William Saroyan: '*Gone With The Wind* keeps me awake at night sometimes – I mean, the quantity of potatoes earned by the talented novelist' (*NLM* 101). As late as 1965 he was boasting that his next novel, *Slattery's Sago Saga*, would make 'G.W.T.W.', as well as *The Great Gatsby*, redundant (*NLM* 241).

O'Nolan thus presents the spectacle of a fantastical, experimental writer – an inheritor of Joyce's modernism – seeking to match the commercial exploits of bestselling authors. The sociologist Pierre Bourdieu argues that modernist literature inverts the world's economic priorities: the less commercial success one earns, the more aesthetic credit accrues. To lose out on economic capital is to win cultural capital.[19] O'Nolan associated the latter with the aestheticism he chose to see in Joyce: in his bid to escape his predecessor, he hoped to trade in aesthetic kudos for 'potatoes' pure and simple. Correspondingly, Myles aims a sharp satirical arrow at the modernist practice of releasing deluxe editions of literary works:

> You know the limited edition ramp. If you write very obscure verse (and why shouldn't you, pray?) for which there is little or no market, you pretend that there is an enormous demand, and that the stuff has to be rationed. Only 300 copies will be printed, you say, and then the type will be broken up for ever. Let the connoisseurs and bibliophiles savage each other for the honour and glory of snatching a copy. Positively no reprint. Reproduction in whole or in part forbidden. Three hundred copies of which this is Number 4,312. Hand-monkeyed oklamon paper, indigo boards in interpulped squirrel-toe, not to mention twelve point Campile Perpetua cast specially for the occasion. Complete, unabridged, and positively unexpurgated. Thirty-five bob a knock and a gory livid bleeding bargain at the price. (*BM* 228)

This accuses limited editions – of which *Ulysses* was paradigmatic – of concealing, or dodging, commercial failure, and mocks the fetishism that they artificially generate. Its cynicism also implies that a deluxe edition is really a commercial strategy masquerading as a refusal of commerce: the inflated price of the limited-edition book manipulates the market more cunningly than Margaret Mitchell herself. In this respect Myles anticipates much later accounts of modernist culture and its deliberate development of economies whose very restriction was lucrative.[20]

Brian O'Nolan, by contrast, set himself to dream of unlimited markets and bestseller status. His major novels failed to achieve this: the closest he came was *Cruiskeen Lawn*, a job of work unmistakably wrapped up in the everyday world, which nonetheless gives vent to O'Nolan's anarchic literary talent. This ambiguous status helps to make the column such a fascinating object: is it modernist epic or mere ephemera?

Or both at once? For we are now as interested in modernism's contingencies as in its absolutes. The closed totality of the great work, the serene self-possession of the well-wrought sentence, even the sublime undecidability of pure text, are less in focus at present than all that surrounds them: railways and telephones, politics and popular culture, publishing houses and the press. Joyce himself now compels attention for the ways he found himself in the *Irish Homestead* or the *Sporting Times*, for the use he made of that grubby, daily world rather than for his ability to rise above it. Flann O'Brien, or Brian O'Nolan, or Myles na gCopaleen, might be the emblem of such an era: an artist who could never really see his writing as art, a novelist who could barely keep a novel from coming undone, a man who, having fallen from the path of writerliness, found it so grindingly difficult to climb out of the world of whiskey and newsprint, into the consolations of mere literature. In one deeply percipient column he registers the uncertain status of his own writing, and hints at the enduring qualities of what seems disposable:

> Always remember that I am writing, not merely passing trash to stuff a small hole in a businessman's day, but also medieval texts to puzzle those who will attend the Institute of Advanced Studies a thousand years hence. Make allowances for the complexity of my task, and be respectful when you are reading what may yet be hailed as one of Ireland's most valuable pre-historic treasures. (*AW* 54)

Notes

INTRODUCTION: THE MORNING AFTER

1. Brian McHale's *Postmodernist Fiction* (London: Routledge, 1987) claims Flann O'Brien as a postmodernist. For his influence on other writers, see Rüdiger Imhof, 'The Presence of Flann O'Brien in Contemporary Fiction', in Anne Clune and Tess Hurson (eds), *Conjuring Complexities: Essays on Flann O'Brien* (Belfast: Institute of Irish Studies), 151–64; Sue Asbee, *Flann O'Brien* (Boston: Twayne, 1991), ch. 8.
2. The most generous synopsis of such work is Declan Kiberd, *Inventing Ireland: The Literature of the Modern Nation* (London: Jonathan Cape, 1995).
3. Hugh Kenner, *The Stoic Comedians* (Berkeley and Los Angeles: University of California Press, 1962), 67.
4. Robert Tracy, Introduction, in Flann O'Brien (Myles na gCopaleen), *Rhapsody in Stephen's Green: The Insect Play* (Dublin: Lilliput, 1994), 2.
5. See Anthony Cronin, *No Laughing Matter: The Life and Times of Flann O'Brien* (London: Grafton, 1969), 200; Peter Costello and Peter van de Kamp, *Flann O'Brien: An Illustrated Biography* (London: Bloomsbury, 1987), 64.
6. Compare Costello and van de Kamp, *Flann O'Brien*, 45–50, and Cronin, *No Laughing Matter*, 67–70.
7. Oscar Wilde, 'The Critic as Artist' (1891), in *The Importance of Being Earnest and Other Writings*, ed. Joseph Bristow (London and New York: Routledge, 1992), 144.
8. Richard Ellmann, *Yeats: The Man and the Masks* (London: Faber, 1961), 175–6.
9. Fredric Jameson, *Postmodernism, or, the Cultural Logic of Late Capitalism* (London: Verso, 1991), 12.
10. Quoted in R. F. Foster, *Modern Ireland 1600–1972* (Harmondsworth: Penguin, 1989), 431.
11. W. B. Yeats, 'The Man and the Echo', in *Collected Poems*, ed. Augustine Martin (London: Vintage, 1992), 361.
12. See Foster, *Modern Ireland*, ch. 18.

13. On the history of independent Ireland, see Foster, *Modern Ireland*, part 4; J. J. Lee, *Ireland 1912–1985: Politics and Society* (Cambridge: Cambridge University Press, 1989); Terence Brown, *Ireland: A Social and Cultural History 1922–1985* (London: Fontana, 1985); Dermot Keogh, *Twentieth-Century Ireland: Nation and State* (Dublin: Gill & Macmillan, 1994).

14. See Brown, *Ireland*, 107, 18.

15. James Joyce, *A Portrait of the Artist as a Young Man*, ed. Seamus Deane (Harmondsworth: Penguin, 1992), 220.

16. See Andrew Gibson, *Joyce's Revenge* (Oxford: Oxford University Press, 2002).

17. The classic work on this is Vivien Mercier, *The Irish Comic Tradition* (Oxford: Clarendon Press, 1962).

CHAPTER 1. YOURS SINCERELY: THE EARLY YEARS

1. T. S. Eliot, *The Waste Land* (1922), in *Collected Poems* (London: Faber, 1974), 63.

2. Eliot, *The Waste Land*, 79.

3. *The Waste Land* had already become a byword in advanced literary circles by the time it received the endorsements of two influential books: in America, Edmund Wilson's *Axel's Castle* (New York: Charles Scribner's Sons, 1931), and in England, F. R. Leavis's *New Bearings in Modern Poetry* (London: Chatto & Windus, 1932). More directly pertinent to O'Nolan is the status that Eliot's work had acquired in literary Dublin by this point. See Alex Davis, 'Reactions from their Burg: Irish Modernist Poets of the 1930s', in Alex Davis and Lee M. Jenkins, *Locations of Literary Modernism: Region and Nation in British and American Modernist Poetry* (Cambridge: Cambridge University Press, 2000), 135–55.

4. See James Joyce, letter to Harriet Shaw Weaver (15 August 1925), in *Selected Letters of James Joyce*, ed. Richard Ellmann (London: Faber, 1975), 309.

5. See John Wilson Foster, *Colonial Consequences: Essays in Irish Literature and Culture* (Dublin: Lilliput, 1991), ch. 14.

6. This detail may find an echo in *At Swim-Two-Birds*, where the character Trellis will only read books with green covers (*AS* 99).

7. See Peter Bürger, *Theory of the Avant-Garde*, trans. Michael Shaw (Manchester: Manchester University Press, 1984).

8. See J. J. Lee, *Ireland 1912–1985: Politics and Society* (Cambridge: Cambridge University Press, 1989), 49.

9. Dermot Keogh, *Twentieth-Century Ireland: Nation and State* (Dublin: Gill & Macmillan, 1994), 104.

10. Lee, *Ireland 1912–1985*, 236.

CHAPTER 2. ODD NUMBERS: *AT SWIM-TWO-BIRDS*

1. The opening chapter heading featured in the first edition, but was initially absent from Penguin's 1967 edition. It has been reinstated in subsequent printings.
2. Sue Asbee, *Flann O'Brien* (Boston: Twayne, 1991), 23.
3. Anthony West, 'Inspired Nonsense', in Rüdiger Imhof (ed.), *Alive Alive O! Flann O'Brien's 'At Swim-Two-Birds'* (Dublin: Wolfhound Press, 1985), 45.
4. I borrow the convenient term 'plain men' from Stephen Knight, 'Forms of Gloom' , in Imhof (ed.), *Alive Alive O!*, 87. The adjective echoes their appreciation of the 'pint of plain' hymned by Jem Casey (*AS* 77).
5. This echoes the idea of cursing, in which words have power to wound: indeed Sweeny's plight is the result of such an act (*AS* 65).
6. Gustave Flaubert, letter to Louis Bouilhet (4 September 1850), in *Selected Letters*, trans. Geoffrey Wall (Harmondsworth: Penguin, 1997), 156.
7. W. B. Yeats, 'The Statues', in *Collected Poems* ed. Augustine Martin (London: Vintage, 1992), 350.
8. Anthony Cronin, 'An Extraordinary Achievement', in Imhof (ed.), *Alive Alive O!*, 111.
9. Bernard Benstock, 'The Three Faces of Brian Nolan', in Imhof (ed.), *Alive Alive O!*, 69.
10. Niall Sheridan, 'Brian, Flann and Myles', in Imhof (ed.), *Alive Alive O!*, 76.
11. Ibid., 72–4.
12. Ibid., 76.

CHAPTER 3. WHAT GOES AROUND: *THE THIRD POLICEMAN*

1. Hugh Kenner, 'The Fourth Policeman', in Anne Clune and Tess Hurson (eds), *Conjuring Complexities: Essays on Flann O'Brien* (Belfast: Institute of Irish Studies, 1997), 70–71.
2. Sue Asbee, *Flann O'Brien* (Boston: Twayne, 1991), 59.
3. Keith Hopper, *Flann O'Brien: A Portrait of the Artist as a Young Postmodernist* (Cork: Cork University Press, 1995).
4. For this tradition, see Margot Gayle Backus, *The Gothic Family Romance: Heterosexuality, Child Sacrifice and the Anglo-Irish Colonial Order* (Durham and London: Duke University Press, 1999). See also Terry Eagleton, *Heathcliffe and the Great Hunger* (London: Verso, 1995), 187–99.
5. We can guess at a link between the novel's cyclical structure and the importance of bicycles within it, though this is not made explicit.

6. See Nicholas J. Wade and Michael Swanston, *Visual Perception: An Introduction* (London and New York: Routledge, 1991), which opens with the claim that 'Vision is our dominant sense' (p. ix).
7. Anne Clune's O'Brien bibliography mentions the script for an Irish film of *The Third Policeman*: appropriately, the film is uncompleted and the script unpublished (Clune and Hurson (eds), *Conjuring Complexities*, 188).
8. See Hugh Kenner, *The Stoic Comedians* (Berkeley and Los Angeles: University of California Press, 1962), 39–41.
9. The most brilliantly extreme version of this ploy is Vladimir Nabokov's *Pale Fire* (1962).
10. Other instances of infinite series in the novel include Anon's 'interminable speculations' that Mathers' real eyes are hidden somewhere behind his visible ones (*TP* 26), and his suspicion that he may be somewhere inside a 'vast sequence of imponderable beings' (*TP* 123).
11. Kenner, 'The Fourth Policeman', 67.

CHAPTER 4. LITERARY FATE: *THE POOR MOUTH*

1. See James Knowlson, *Damned To Fame: The Life of Samuel Beckett* (London: Bloomsbury, 1996), 293–5, 357. Anne Clissmann describes *An Béal Bocht* as an English translation retranslated back into Irish (*FOB* 240), an idea which echoes the inter-linguistic movement of Beckett's prose.
2. Quoted in Jane Farnon, 'Motifs of Gaelic Lore and Literature in *An Béal Bocht*', in Anne Clune and Tess Hurson (eds), *Conjuring Complexities: Essays on Flann O'Brien* (Belfast: Institute of Irish Studies, 1997), 109.
3. See Declan Kiberd, *Inventing Ireland* (London: Jonathan Cape, 1995), 136–54.
4. Farnon, 'Motifs', 89.
5. Ibid., 102–6.
6. See Sue Asbee, *Flann O'Brien* (Boston: Twayne, 1991), 71.
7. Ibid., 72.
8. Kiberd, *Inventing Ireland*, 511.
9. See Farnon, 'Motifs', 96.
10. Kiberd, *Inventing Ireland*, 504–10.

CHAPTER 5. THE ENDS OF NARRATIVE: *THE HARD LIFE* AND *THE DALKEY ARCHIVE*

1. Tess Hurson, 'Conspicuous Absences: *The Hard Life*', in Anne Clune and Tess Hurson (eds), *Conjuring Complexities: Essays on Flann O'Brien* (Belfast: Institute of Irish Studies, 1997), 119.
2. Ibid., 120.

3. Ibid., 128.
4. Ibid., 120.
5. See, for instance, Sue Asbee, *Flann O'Brien* (Boston: Twayne, 1991), 85.
6. Letter to Grant Richards (15 October 1905), *Selected Letters of James Joyce*, ed. Richard Ellmann (London: Faber, 1975), 79.
7. Niall Sheridan, 'Brian, Flann and Myles', in Rüdiger Imhof (ed.), *Alive Alive O! Flann O'Brien's 'At Swim-Two-Birds'* (Dublin: Wolfhound Press, 1985), 74.
8. Keith Hopper, *Flann O'Brien: A Portrait of the Artist as a Young Post-modernist* (Cork: Cork University Press, 1995), ch. 2.
9. See Asbee, *Flann O'Brien*, 87; Hopper, *Flann O'Brien*, 64.
10. Hopper, *Flann O'Brien*, 63.
11. Ibid., 71.
12. It is possible that O'Nolan drew not just on the *Third Policeman* typescript of 1939, but also on other material that he had first drafted later in the 1940s. Biographers have pointed out that certain anachronisms in the novel – the fact that trams are still running to Dalkey, for instance – place it in the late 1940s (*NLM* 229; *IB* 130). The novel does hint at a past setting, referring to 'the time of these events' as though distinct from the present (*DA* 100); but it is never explicit. The fact that 1 September falls on a Saturday (*DA* 89) tantalizingly suggests 1945 or 1951, but may simply reflect the time of composition (1962).
13. Asbee, *Flann O'Brien*, 105.
14. James Joyce, *A Portrait of the Artist as a Young Man*, ed. Seamus Deane (Harmondsworth: Penguin, 1992), 240, 276.
15. See Wayne C. Booth, *The Rhetoric of Fiction* (Chicago: Chicago University Press, 1961), 324–36.
16. Asbee, *Flann O'Brien*, 105.
17. For an exceedingly generous reading, see Thomas F. Shea, *Flann O'Brien's Exorbitant Novels* (Lewisburg: Bucknell University Press, 1992), 154–6.
18. Ibid., 152–67.
19. For a picture, see Peter Costello and Peter van de Kamp, *Flann O'Brien: An Illustrated Biography* (London: Bloomsbury, 1987), 122.
20. See Asbee, *Flann O'Brien*, 103.

CHAPTER 6. LOCAL UNAESTHETIC: *CRUISKEEN LAWN*

1. Declan Kiberd, *Inventing Ireland* (London: Jonathan Cape, 1995), 512.
2. Hugh Kenner, *A Colder Eye: The Modern Irish Writers* (London: Allen Lane, 1983), 257.

3. Seamus Deane, *A Short History of Irish Literature* (London: Hutchinson, 1986), 199.
4. Benstock, 'The Three Faces of Brian Nolan', in Rüdiger Imhof (ed.), *Alive Alive O! Flann O'Brien's 'At Swim-Two-Birds'* (Dublin: Wolfhound Press, 1985), 59.
5. Kiberd, *Inventing Ireland*, 512.
6. Steven Young, 'Fact/Fiction: *Cruiskeen Lawn*, 1945–1966', in Anne Clune and Tess Hurson (eds), *Conjuring Complexities: Essays on Flann O'Brien* (Belfast: Institute of Irish Studies, 1997), 116, 118.
7. Ibid., 118.
8. T. S. Eliot, '*Ulysses*, Order and Myth' (1923), in *Selected Prose*, ed. Frank Kermode (London: Faber, 1975), 177.
9. Kiberd, *Inventing Ireland*, 498.
10. See Jack White, 'Myles, Flann and Brian', in Timothy O'Keeffe (ed.), *Myles: Portraits of Brian O'Nolan* (London: Martin Brian and O'Keeffe, 1973), 63.
11. Kiberd, *Inventing Ireland*, 499.
12. O'Nolan would surely have been glad of the recognition from his American contemporary S. J. Perelman, never mind his spelling of 'na Gopaleen'. See *Don't Tread On Me: The Selected Letters of S. J. Perelman*, ed. Prudence Crowther (Harmondsworth: Penguin, 1988), 233. For an eyewitness account of the birth of Myles, see Tony Gray, *The Lost Years: The Emergency in Ireland 1939–1945* (London: Little, Brown, 1997), 110–11.
13. Anthony Cronin, 'Squalid Exegesis', in Clune and Hurson (eds), *Conjuring Complexities*, 38.
14. See Kenner, *A Colder Eye*, 258–9.
15. Young, 'Fact/Fiction', 116.
16. Niall Sheridan, 'Brian, Flann and Myles', in Imhof (ed.), *Alive Alive O!*, 74.
17. Young, 'Fact/Fiction', 117.
18. For discussions of *Ulysses* and newspapers, see Steven Connor, *James Joyce* (Plymouth: Northcote House, 1996), ch. 4, and Declan Kiberd, *Irish Classics* (London: Faber, 2000), ch. 26.
19. See Pierre Bourdieu, *The Field of Cultural Production* (Oxford: Blackwell, 1993), ch. 1.
20. See Lawrence Rainey, *Institutions of Modernism* (New Haven: Yale University Press, 1998).

Select Bibliography

WORKS BY BRIAN O'NOLAN

At Swim-Two-Birds (1939; Harmondsworth: Penguin, 1967). O'Brien's first novel: a dazzling fictional spree, influential on later generations of writers.

The Third Policeman (1967; London: Flamingo, 1993). Rejected by Longman in 1940 and unpublished until after O'Nolan's death: a major work, whose rejection and secret existence evidently weighed heavily on him.

The Poor Mouth, trans. Patrick C. Power (1941; London: Flamingo, 1993). A satire on the rural Gaelic memoir, written in Irish and published under the name 'Myles na gCopaleen'; translated posthumously.

The Hard Life (1961; London: Picador, 1976). A slim comic novel which commenced O'Nolan's late return to writing fiction.

The Dalkey Archive (1964; London: Flamingo, 1993). An uneven work which revisits motifs from the then unpublished *Third Policeman*, and concludes O'Nolan's struggle with the legacy of James Joyce.

Stories and Plays (1973; London: Paladin, 1991). Includes the unfinished novel *Slattery's Sago Saga* (*c.* 1964), the political play *Faustus Kelly* (1943) and the significant essay on Joyce, 'A Bash in the Tunnel' (1951), among other short pieces.

Rhapsody in Stephen's Green: The Insect Play, ed. Robert Tracy (Dublin: Lilliput, 1994). A political satire produced in 1943 and published for the first time in the 1990s.

The Best of Myles, ed. Kevin O'Nolan (1968; London: Picador, 1977). A generous selection from the *Cruiskeen Lawn* column, made by O'Nolan's brother, this volume did much for Myles' posthumous international reputation. It is drawn from the first five years of the column.

Further Cuttings from Cruiskeen Lawn (1976; London: Grafton, 1988). A second selection from the column, mainly covering the period

1947–1957, but also including the first column (October 1940); includes significant social and political commentary.

The Hair of the Dogma (1976; London: Grafton, 1993). Another selection from *Cruiskeen Lawn*, which covers the same period as *Further Cuttings*.

A Flann O'Brien Reader, ed. Stephen Jones (New York: Viking, 1978). An extensive selection of material from different phases of O'Nolan's career, including the important *Cruiskeen Lawn* series 'The Autobiography of Myles na gCopaleen'.

Myles Away From Dublin, ed. Martin Green (1985; London: Flamingo, 1993). A collection of columns written under the name George Knowall, which first appeared in the *Nationalist and Leinster Times* from 1960 to 1966.

Myles Before Myles, ed. John Wyse Jackson (London: Grafton, 1988). An important collection which makes available much of the brilliant early writing from *Comhthrom Féinne* and *Blather*.

Flann O'Brien at War: Myles na gCopaleen 1940–1945, ed. John Wyse Jackson (London: Duckworth, 1999). A new selection of previously unpublished wartime writings, joined together by the editor into a self-consciously tenuous narrative.

WORKS ON BRIAN O'NOLAN

Asbee, Sue, *Flann O'Brien* (Boston: Twayne, 1991). A succinct introduction which makes good use of O'Nolan's letters.

Booker, M. Keith. *Flann O'Brien, Bakhtin, and Menippean Satire* (Syracuse, NY: Syracuse University Press, 1995). A study which places the fiction in comparative and theoretical contexts.

Chace, William M., 'Joyce and Flann O'Brien', *Eire-Ireland*, 22:4 (Winter 1987), 140–52. An account of O'Nolan's ambivalent relation to Joyce.

Clissmann, Anne, *Flann O'Brien: A Critical Introduction to his Writings* (Dublin: Gill & Macmillan, 1975). An early, comprehensive treatment of O'Nolan's work.

Clune, Anne, and Tess Hurson (eds), *Conjuring Complexities: Essays on Flann O'Brien* (Belfast: Institute of Irish Studies, 1997). A collection loosely based on the 1986 Symposium; includes the fullest primary and secondary bibliographies thus far.

Cronin, Anthony, *Dead as Doornails: Bohemian Dublin in the Fifties and Sixties* (London and Dublin: Calder and Boyers/Dolmen Press, 1976). Contains memories of O'Nolan alongside Behan and Kavanagh.

———*No Laughing Matter: The Life and Times of Flann O'Brien* (London: Grafton, 1989). The fullest biographical account available; indispensable for a full picture of O'Nolan.

Curran, Steven. ' "No, This is Not From *The Bell*": Brian O'Nolan's 1943 *Cruiskeen Lawn* Anthology', *Éire-Ireland*, 32:2 and 3 (Summer/ Fall 1997), 79–92. Places an early *Cruiskeen Lawn* collection in its historical context.

Hopper, Keith, *Flann O'Brien: A Portrait of the Artist as a Young Post-modernist* (Cork: Cork University Press, 1995). An ambitious attempt to combine Formalist, post-colonial and feminist perspectives, which focuses particularly on *The Third Policeman*.

Imhof, Rüdiger (ed.), *Alive Alive O! Flann O'Brien's 'At Swim-Two-Birds'* (Dublin: Wolfhound Press, 1985). A judicious collection of essays on the novel, reaching back to O'Nolan's own earliest comments on it and contemporary reviews.

Kiberd, Declan, *Inventing Ireland: The Literature of the Modern Nation* (London: Jonathan Cape, 1995). This major work on post-colonial Ireland devotes a chapter to *The Poor Mouth*.

Ó'Conaire, Breandán, *Myles na Gaelige* (Dublin: An Clóchomhar, 1986). A study of O'Nolan's work in Irish.

O'Keeffe, Timothy (ed.), *Myles: Portraits of Brian O'Nolan* (London: Martin Brian and O'Keeffe, 1973). An early collection of biographical reminiscences.

Powell, David, 'An Annotated Bibliography of Myles na gCopaleen's "Cruiskeen Lawn" Commentaries on James Joyce', *James Joyce Quarterly*, 9:1 (Fall 1971), 50–62. A useful guide to O'Nolan's often dismissive references to Joyce in the *Irish Times*.

Ryan, John, *Remembering How We Stood: Bohemian Dublin at the Mid-Century* (Dublin: Gill and Macmillan, 1975). Memoir including a chapter on 'The Incomparable Myles'.

Shea, Thomas F., *Flann O'Brien's Exorbitant Novels* (Lewisburg: Bucknell University Press, 1992). A study of the novels, and some of the early writings, which draws on manuscript research.

Spencer, Andrew, 'Many Worlds: The New Physics in Flann O'Brien's *The Third Policeman*', *Éire-Ireland*, 30:1 (Spring 1995), 145–58. A treatment of the novel in the context of twentieth-century science.

Index

O'Leary, Peter (Laoghaire,
    Peadar), 64, 68
O'Madan, The, 24
O'Nolan, Brian, see O'Brien,
    Flann
    Myles Before Myles, 3
O'Nolan, Ciarán, 18–19
O'Nolan, Evelyn (née
    McDonnell), 46
Ó Nualláin, Brían, see O'Nolan,
    Brian
O'Ruddy, Jno., 24

Parnell, Charles Stewart, 8, 10
Pearse, Patrick, 8, 41, 62
Plain People of Ireland, 95–7, 101
Pound, Ezra, 16–17
Power, Patrick C., 61, 63
Puck Fare, 103

Razzle, 19

Saint Augustine, 78, 84
Saroyan, William, 46, 47, 106
Sayers, Peig, 64
Shaw, George Bernard, 92
Shea, Thomas F., 85

Sheridan, Niall, 11, 19, 41–4
Smyllie, R.M., 87
'South American Joe', 24
Sporting Times, 108
Synge, John Millington, 17–18,
    65, 94
    Riders to the Sea, 65

Time, 6
Tracy, Robert, 4

Ungerland, Clara, 6
Upshott, Hilda, 24

van de Kamp, Peter, 72

West, Anthony, 34
'West-Briton Nationalist', 62
White, Jack, 89
Wilde, Oscar, 6–7, 24

Yeats, W.B., 2, 6–7, 9–10, 15, 17,
    40–1, 103
    'The Man and the Echo', 10
    'The Statues', 41
Young, Steven M., 88, 102–3